Heartwarming Soft Toys

Kay Duggins

CHILTON BOOK COMPANY
Radnor, Pennsylvania

Library of Congress Catalog Card No. 85-61159
ISBN 0-8019-7708-8
Manufactured in the United States of America

1 2 3 4 5 6 7 8 9 0   4 3 2 1 0 9 8 7 6 5

To my mother, who never allowed me to say, "I can't."
To my husband, who always said, "You can!"
To my children for their inspiration and honest opinions.
To my friends for cheering me on.

Acknowledgement

I didn't think of myself as a writer, but some very special people at THE MOTHER EARTH NEWS made me feel like one. Heartfelt thanks to editor Bobbi Henderson. She did the hard part and made work a pleasure for me. Thanks to David Dyer for believing that I could be an author. With their guidance, I was given the chance to try. To the people listed below—layout artists, photographers, proofreaders, and all others who helped with the production of this book, I offer sincere thanks. This work would not have been possible without team effort.

Spanky Alexander
Patricia Anderson
Jennifer Brock
Clark Center
Ken Cross
Marsha Drake
Kenneth Forsgren
Carolyn Frederick

Jack Green
Steve Keull
Keith Roddy
Sherry Seagle
Carolyn Sizemore
Kay Holmes Stafford
Emily Stetson
Mark Wilson

Susan Myking Wood

TABLE OF
CONTENTS

Designs

Introduction

Are you new to the world of toymaking? If so, welcome, come on in, and pull up a chair. You are about to embark on a hobby that is literally child's play. I want to show you how to make simple, washable, lovable, huggable toys for the little ones—or not so little ones—in your life.

Toymaking has invaluable rewards—feeling the joy of creating, seeing a child's eyes light up, receiving a thank-you hug. These are satisfactions that money can't buy.

I began designing toys for my children because I had scraps of fabric on hand. It was a costless venture that took only a little time. As my children grew, I discovered that I was getting as much pleasure from designing toys as they were from playing with them. Now, twenty years later, I still get excited each time a new design comes to life.

Soft toys are primarily toys made from a wide range of fabrics and stuffed with polyester fiberfill or any other safe stuffing. They can be as simple as you like or as intricate as a fine work of art. Created by loving hands, a toy given to a child or an adult becomes a one-of-a-kind treasure. There's something magical about a soft toy; I think the recipient senses the love that's tucked inside.

The most beautiful toy is worn and frazzled with love. It has shared confidences and has been dragged, wagged, hugged, squeezed, and slept with over the years. What memories that soft little body must hold. It's a good friend, becoming more treasured with the passing of time.

You can make toys filled with love, too; I know you can. Together, let's try.

How-To Hints: Tools, Materials, & Techniques

Small children don't need fancy, busy toys. It's much better to give them soft, simple-featured toys that let them use their own imaginations. Softness of a toy is important; it invites a hug. In this country and around the world, people are rediscovering the treasured crafts of the past: quilting, lacemaking, stenciling—the list is endless. Let's add toymaking up there at the top of the list of rediscovered crafts. I can think of no craft that is more rewarding or less costly to undertake.

Soft toys are as varied as the artists who create them. I have seen some soft toys that are astonishingly realistic. You'd almost think they could breathe. Then there are soft sculpture toys so abstract that I question their being categorized as toys. Toys are created for all ages. Some fall into the category of play toys, and some exist for the sheer enjoyment of us older kids as collectibles or reminders of our past.

I have wondered why more people don't try their hands at toymaking. In looking for answers, I asked these questions: Do you hate enlarging pictures from graphs? (Yuck, I hate it too!) Do you hate all the darts on those tiny little pattern pieces? (Me, too.) Do you hate the number of pattern pieces required to create a design? Do you hate all those curves and gussets and seams that never ease the way they're supposed to? (It seems too much like work, and toymaking is supposed to be fun.)

Maybe you think you don't know how to stuff. That's okay; with a little practice, you can do a terrific job of stuffing. I recommend starting on an easy, basic pattern and working up to the more advanced patterns as your skills improve. The patterns in this book can be made easily by anyone with even a moderate amount of sewing expertise. Many are for the beginner.

This chapter contains basic information that will help you work efficiently and make attractive toys. You will find how-to hints on materials, tools, techniques, and procedures. Take what works for you, and don't be overly concerned with the rest! One of my main motivations in sharing these designs is to encourage toymakers to use my tested ideas and methods as springboards to new creations.

TOOLS FOR TOYMAKING

If you have done any sewing, you probably have the basic sewing tools that are useful in toymaking. Assemble everything before you begin, as doing so will save time once you start. A sewing basket or box is handy for keeping supplies together. Also helpful is an uncluttered, quiet area where you can spread out your work and let it stay until a project is completed.

Sewing machine: This piece of equipment is not absolutely required (soft toys used to be made by hand), but toymaking is much faster and easier when you do as much as possible by machine.

Scissors: Regular sewing scissors, good sharp ones, make cutting both patterns and material easier.

Needles: Sewing baskets usually contain needles of various sizes for basic sewing. You'll want sharps for hand sewing, crewel for embroidery, and some big ones for sewing with yarn.

Blunt dowel or knitting needle: Either of these can be an invaluable aid for turning and stuffing toys. I use a 3/8″ wooden dowel about 18″ long. Be sure to round off the ends and sand them smooth, so as not to snag the material.

Tracing paper & brown wrapping paper: You will need these for pattern-making. Tracing paper is also known as dressmaker's carbon.

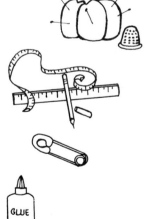

Straight pins: Use to anchor pattern pieces on fabric during cutting.

Thimble: My mother insists this is a necessity, but I have never learned to use one. I say it's optional.

Tape measure & ruler: These will be used in many ways.

Pencil & tailor's chalk: Use for marking material.

Safety pins: Safety pins can be used to thread elastic or ribbon through casings.

Glue: White clear-drying glue can be used for attaching felt features, pom-poms, and other trim, unless the toy is for a very small child.

Pinking shears: You may already have these for general sewing. In toymaking, pinking shears are handy for finishing edges, in lieu of hemming or turning.

SEW WHAT?

Before buying any material for toymaking, look around your home. Do you have scraps left over from a sewing project? Most of us have a ragbag full of outgrown or worn-out clothing. Towels that are frayed around the edges, but that still have some thick spots left can be used in toymaking. Socks, whether men's or children's, can be turned into toys. Even panty hose can be used to make lifelike characters.

When my mother was busy sewing, she would sometimes let me go through the button bag to pick out the buttons to use on what she was making. It was fun to have the responsibility for choosing which buttons would look best.

Any garment that is useless in its present state might be considered for recycling into toys. For instance, around our house we have a number of "divorced" (without a mate) gloves and socks. Worn-out or outgrown clothes, frayed or stained linen, old insulated underwear or sleepwear can be used in toymaking. One of the great things about recycling these items is that the items will otherwise go unused. With a little imagination, a bit of trim, and a heaping portion of love, a treasured toy can be created.

If you don't have a sewing machine, or if you don't like to sew on a machine or any other way, you'll find that using old clothing is a fast, fun-filled way to make toys with a minimum of work. Sleeves or pant legs are ready-made fabric tubes that invite soft-stuffing. By closing the ends and adding trim, you've got a toy. Soft-stuff several sleeve or leg tubes, close the ends, and stitch the tubes together to form any number of toy designs. Children's clothes can provide small tubes, while adults' clothes offer bigger tubes; you can mix and match for more versatility (see the illustration).

The seams in used clothing don't have to be a problem—play them up. People will think you put the seam there purposely. If a garment is threadbare in spots, patch the worn area and use the patch as a toy's focal point.

Always make sure that any fabric used in toymaking is clean. If there's doubt, wash it again.

After reading this book, you may be able to look around your home and see rags ready to be turned into riches. Toymaking can be a monetarily rewarding hobby, but there are even greater rewards: the pleasure you receive by giving a toy you've made, and the joy of watching a scrap of fabric, odd pieces of trim, and some stuffing evolve into a three-dimensional creation that you can see, feel, and share.

CHOOSING THE RIGHT FABRIC AND PRINT

In pairing your proposed toy with a fabric, coordinate the size of the toy with the size of the print. Tiny toys usually look best in small-scale prints or in solids. Larger toys can go bolder. Be adventurous. Experiment.

Striped or plaid fabrics generally don't appeal to me, but if a particular design looks as if it would work in a stripe or plaid, I'll try it. Flexibility and freedom in mixing and matching fabrics, trims, and features will add to the individuality and charm of a toy design. In garment-making, if you choose the wrong fabric or fail to follow the instructions closely, the finished product may prove unwearable, no matter how many extra touches you add. Keep this parallel in mind as you make toys. Always follow the basic rules of safe and sturdy construction. Then after assuring yourself of a well-made toy, you are free to veer from the basics to develop your own innovative designs.

THE STUFF THAT TOYS ARE MADE OF

The stuffing I recommend is polyester fiberfill. It's snowy-white, lightweight, washable, quick-drying, and nonallergenic. A one-pound bag is enough to fill several small toys. It's easy to work with and makes a smooth stuffing. I'd like to comment on some other stuffings, however.

Shredded foam is a lightweight, inexpensive, and soft filler, especially for thicker fabrics such as fake fur or terry cloth. It is usually yellowish or flecked with color. For bean bags, it's good to mix it with styrene beads or aquarium gravel. If you have never used shredded foam before, prepare yourself: It's MESSY. Those little flakes come alive! They cling to your hands, arms, clothes, carpet, and furniture. And once you start working in it, just pray that the phone doesn't ring; this is one job you can't quit in the middle of! When I used this stuffing, it was the most un-fun part of my toymaking.

Cotton is not used in toymaking to the degree it once was. It tends to pack down and lump up. In my opinion, it can't compare to polyester fiberfill.

Old hose make a good stuffing for beginners to use in toymaking. Don't throw away panty hose with runs. Wash, dry, and cut them into small pieces. Then store them in a box or bag. You'll be surprised at how fast a stockpile of stuffing can build. Be sure to cut the material into small pieces or strips, so it will give a smoother stuff. Remember, this filler has the advantage of being free.

Never use seeds or grains as a filler in toys: You would be inviting insect infestation as well as mold.

For more information on stuffing toys successfully, see the tips listed below.

Stuffing Tips

● *Practice* stuffing.

● A soft, lightweight toy invites a hug.

● The quality of the stuffing will determine the quality of the finished toy's appearance.

● Stuff extremities first, using a dowel to push stuffing into small areas and constantly feeling to determine where stuffing is needed.

● The degree of softness depends upon a toy's style and upon how much stuffing must be used to retain that toy's shape.

● It is difficult to go back and fill out a spot after the toy is stuffed, so pack the filling smoothly as you go.

● Never wad the stuffing. Stuff by "strands" (this applies to polyester fiberfill stuffing).

● Toys tend to pack down after being played with for a while, but it's better to add more stuffing later than to stuff the toy tight at first. Soft toys should be just that—*soft*, not heavy or hard.

FACIAL FEATURES

Cartoons, comic strips, and coloring books show examples of simple lines being used effectively for maximum conveyance of emotion. Take a lesson from these sources as you try to create pleasing facial expressions for your soft toys. An expression *can* be a simple combination of circles for eyes and straight lines for the nose and mouth, but an expression that conveys some happiness can favorably influence a child's feeling about himself and his toy.

Facial features can be successfully produced with embroidery (see pages 14 and 28), appliqué, fabric paint (be sure it's nontoxic and washable), or glued-on trims—felt, pompoms, rickrack, etc. Rely on your own judgment of what method of face-making is appropriate for a particular toy. If you choose to do machine appliqué, the face must be appliquéd before you stitch the body together. All other features can be added after the body is stuffed.

Toys and dolls are more childlike in appearance when the features correspond to the proportions of a real child's face. Try the following simple tips: Place the features lower on the face. Find the center of the face by dividing it in half horizontally and vertically. (See the illustration.) Position the eyes just below the horizontal center line and to either side of the vertical center line. A wide-eyed look is appealing, but don't place the eyes *too* far apart. Remember that toymaking is an art form that benefits from selective exaggeration. You can emphasize or eliminate any feature you want to—whatever accomplishes the effect you're after. Dare to experiment. Throughout this book you can see how few lines and circles are needed to achieve pleasing expressions. You will notice frequent use of the heart shape. For me, this is the most important shape used in toymaking. Children respond to this shape, and it can be used subtly or boldly. Study the various ways that this heart shape has been used in the section on designs. A little heart can give a creation a big boost.

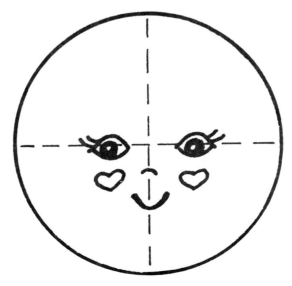

EMBROIDERY STITCHES USED IN THIS BOOK

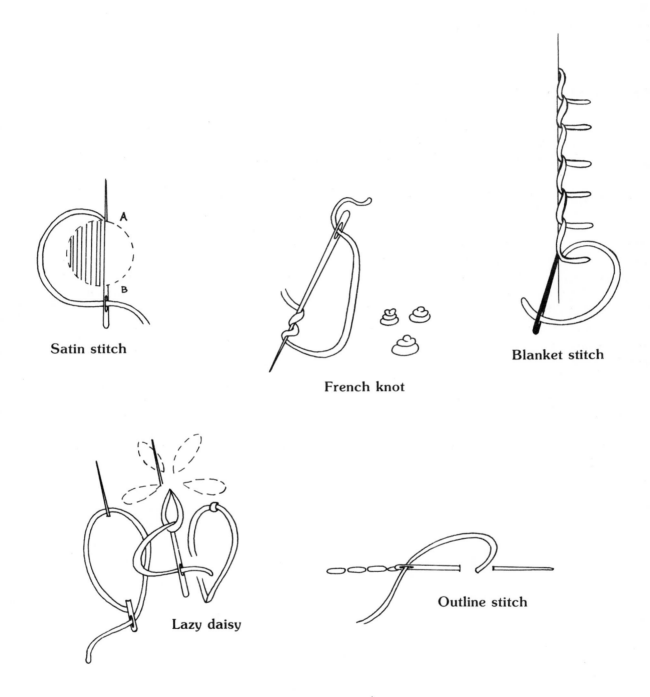

Satin stitch

French knot

Blanket stitch

Lazy daisy

Outline stitch

NOTE: Directions for appliqué will not be given for toys. If you choose to appliqué by machine, do so before pattern pieces are sewn together. To appliqué by hand, you should use the blanket stitch. You'll find this is easier to do after the toy is stuffed.

HAIR-RAISING IDEAS

Hair may be applied to toys/dolls in a variety of ways. There are many new fibers available to use as hair. Check with your local crafts shop. Listed here are some commonly used methods of application. A few are too time-consuming for my taste, but if you enjoy making and attaching hair in this manner, feel free to do so.

Yarn

Fringe: Wind yarn around a piece of cardboard of the width desired. Push off the loops, and stitch through the center on the machine. This creates a fringe which is then stitched to the doll's head along the previous line of machine stitching. Continue to wind and stitch to the length desired.

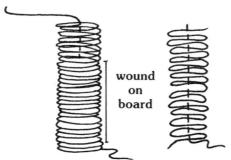

wound
on
board

Lock-and-Loop: Probably the most popular rag doll ever made, the Raggedy Ann, has hair attached with the lock-and-loop method. Lines are marked on the head, as a stitch guide. Thread a needle with one strand of yarn. Start by leaving an end of thread extended a few inches (about the length of the loops you plan to make). Take a short stitch through the head. Take the next stitch and leave a loop. Next, stitch and pull through taut. Continue. The stitches are placed side by side along the stitch lines. The stitch that is pulled through snugly is the lock; the next stitch is the loop.

stitching line

side view

Braids: A full head of hair is not required for a doll with a hat stitched to the head, but you might want to add a braid to frame the face. The length of yarn and number of strands will depend upon the doll's size. Measure and cut lengths of yarn. Tie a ribbon an inch or so from one end. Divide the strands into three even bunches, braid to the other end, and tie a ribbon the same distance from the second end as you did at the beginning. Fold the braid in half to find the center, and tack the braid to the center top front of the head. Stitch the braid securely to the head.

Bangs: Measure the length desired and double. Tie strands in the center and fold down. A few strands of yarn may be all that are required for a small doll. Use more strands for larger dolls. Tie tightly in the center and fold ends together. Tack the tied center to the head. Trim ends of bangs evenly.

"Doggy Ears": This method starts similarly to the fringe method. Measure the length of hair desired and wind hair loops that width. Use bias tape or a strip of paper as a width guide to which you attach the hair. This guide will serve as the part in the doll's hair. Find the center of the length of yarn, lay it along the bias strip, and feed the yarn evenly through the machine. Backstitch at the beginning and the end. At the desired length on either side of the center hair part, tie the hair. Tack the hair (along center machine stitching) to the center of the head and also at the points where the hair is tied. Cut ends of hair evenly.

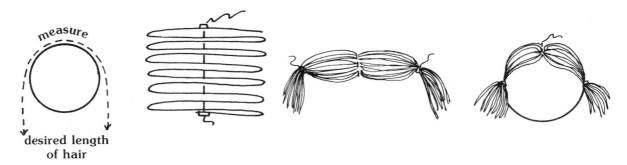

Fabric Rectangles

To make the hair for our clowns, Mr. Hugs and Mrs. Kisses, we used pinking shears to cut 2″ X 5″ rectangles of red cotton fabric. Pinch the center, and then wrap thread around and stitch the center. Stitch to the head at one-inch intervals. This method achieves a bushy head of hair with a minimum of work. For a large rag doll, narrow strips of fabric in hair colors could be substituted for yarn.

Macramé Cord

Some synthetic fibers used in macramé cord can be combed out to be fluffy, and these are great for hair. Used on Skinny Minnie as her arms and legs, cord was left in the rope form with knots tied in the ends to prevent raveling. Another color of macramé cord was used as hair, by simply tacking the cord securely to the head stitching at the sides, and combing out the ends. I prefer this cord to wool or acrylic yarn for some toys.

Felt

Felt can be flat-stitched to pillow shapes to appear as hair, or strips and shapes can be stitched into seams. It's not recommended to use on toys that are for tiny tots, because it isn't as washable or durable as some other materials.

Yo-Yo's

Grandma made quilts from these little round circles of fabric. Yo-yo's are versatile in toymaking. Handstitched closely together onto the head, they make interesting hair. Yo-yo's enhance the soft look of toys. For a pillow-shaped toy such as a lamb, stitch yo-yo's over the body to give a wooly appearance (see illustration). They make attractive (also soft and safe) "buttons" for clown costumes.

 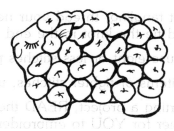

HINTS, HINTS, AND MORE HINTS

● Never use straight pins or other sharp objects in or on anything classified as a child's soft toy.

● All attachments—whether for body construction, features, or trim—should be secured by stitching or gluing.

● Rule of thumb for fabrics with nap: Lay all pattern pieces in the same direction. (Nap is the downy texture of a woven fabric.) To determine if fabric is napped, gently run flat hand in one direction, then the other. If there is nap, fabric will lie down smooth in one direction, but will appear or feel rough if stroked in the other direction.

● Felt has no right or wrong side, and it can be cut in any direction.

● Felt can be stitched on the outside. There's no need to turn the seams in, because the edges do not ravel.

● If you're using felt in the body construction of a toy, do not overstuff. Tight areas will wear thin.

● No one likes a sourpuss, so supply toy faces with smiles, to reflect a happy attitude.

● Give names to the toys you make; we give names to things we care about.

● Get creative with texture and color.

● Use those scraps! Old clothes and worn-out jeans can still lead useful lives. (Save the buttons to use elsewhere.)

● Men's cotton work socks are fantastic for building toys. Using the terry-lined ones wrong side out provides wonderful texture.

● Infants' and children's socks make darling baby dolls, chicks, or bunnies.

● A crochet hook or knitting needle is useful in turning and getting the stuffing into hard-to-reach areas.

● Grocery bags are good for drawing patterns on.

● Infant toys don't have to be in soft colors; circus colors can be fun.

- Embroidered or painted faces should be created after the toy is stuffed. That way, embroidery thread can be hidden in the stuffing, not mashed between stuffing and fabric.

- Always knot TWICE. Do not cut the thread at the knot; take the needle back into the fabric and out away from the knot before cutting.

- For a more professional appearance, match your thread to your fabric in color and weight. A medium-weight cotton or cotton-covered thread #50 or #60 works well in toymaking.

- Set your machine at about 12 stitches per inch for general toymaking.

- To prevent tangling, thread your needle with the end of the thread that came off the spool first and tie the knot in the end that came off the spool last.

- To baste, use eight or less stitches per inch.

- For small items or tighter stitches, use 15 stitches per inch.

- Before starting a project, READ the instructions before deciding when to work the face. Is it easier for YOU to embroider, paint, or appliqué before or after the body is assembled? It's your choice.

- If you don't have fabric or felt in the colors I've suggested, DON'T run out to buy any. Instead, first look around to see what you have on hand, and feel free to substitute.

- If you plan to trace the face from a pattern, lay out the material, with wrong sides together to be cut. Cut out the pattern pieces. Before removing the pattern from the fabric, insert tracing carbon face down between the pattern and the top layer of fabric. With a ball point pen, trace the face onto the fabric.

- In embroidering soft toys, DON'T pull the threads too tight.

- Reinforce all stress points by double-stitching.

- When cutting pattern pieces from fake fur, don't give it a hair cut! Spread the fur away from the cutting line, and cut the backing material with the tip of the scissors. Take small snips.

- Use 1/4" seams for all toy construction, unless otherwise stated.

- Backstitch at the start and finish of all seams; it helps to prevent raveling.

- Clip curves *almost* to stitching, being careful *not* to cut stitching thread.

Heartfelt Notes & Anecdotes

Toys have been with us throughout the ages. They reflect much of a people's culture and have been constructed of a variety of materials, limited only by the imagination and the creative hands. For instance, the list of materials used has run the gamut from bone to polystyrene.

♡

Soft toys should not be limited to a certain age group. What may have been designed for a particular age group may appeal to another. The only stipulation to this generalization involves safety: safety first in toymaking, no matter what the age. Never give a child a toy that's not safe for him or her to play with. You must make that decision.

♡

Remember the heart. That's something to be used in toymaking from day one. Toys are made with love for those we love to love.

♡

Included in this book is the pattern for Bell-Ve-Deer, a reindeer made from men's white cotton terry-lined work socks. When I first made Bell and other sock toys, before I began buying direct from the factory, I bought socks at retail stores. On one particular day, my cart was mounded up with nothing but socks as I was waiting in line at the check-out counter. Suddenly, before I realized what was happening, several ladies converged on my cart and began grabbing my socks! One woman finally took a moment from her rummaging to inquire, "Are these on special?"

Calmly I replied, "No." And sheepishly, the women returned the socks.

♡

First toys should be small enough for little ones to grasp. Babies put everything into their mouths, especially when teething, so make toys out of washable fabrics. Do not use buttons, pins, or trim that could be pulled off and put in their mouths. Keep the toy shape basic and the features simple. I recommend embroidery or appliqué for the face. Use a minimum of felt, since infant toys are washed frequently.

♡

When our daughters were small, I suffered from an affliction called "pack-rat-itis." As with many young families starting out, money was always short in supply but high in demand. Since I did not work outside the home, I felt it my duty to waste as little as possible. If something had outlived its usefulness in one form, I saved it until I could think of another way to use it. As I look back, I am really grateful for those years, because I was challenged to learn design, and I received the satisfaction of knowing that I was helping to provide for our family.

You can always spot a mother of young children—she's the one with her shoestrings tied in a double knot!

♡

Just think of the countless number of snowflakes that have fallen, and yet no two are ever alike. As a mother, I have found it to be even more astounding that whether we have one or a dozen children, no two are ever the same. Each little person from his first moment of life is unique, endowed with his or her own special qualities and traits. How boring it would be if we were all the same!

♡

I can't believe it! I've reached grandmotherhood and lived to tell about it. And I have already figured out that grandchildren are our reward for raising our children.

♡

Once when we were making a sculptured doll design, I was buying infant shoes and clothes for our dolls. I purchased all of the size two shoes in the store and two carts full of size nine-month infant clothes. A lady who had been quietly eyeing my cart's contents finally questioned, "Do you have quintuplets? Or do you run an orphanage for babies who are all the same size?"

♡

Toddling is such a delightful age of discovery! The world is so inviting, and toddlers love to take a "friend" along on their adventures. Soft toy "friends" should be a bit larger than infants' toys. Flatsy-pillow shapes are easily made and make great sleepytime pals. For draggability, add long arms and/or long legs. If your toddler still puts things into his or her mouth, remember: no buttons or trim that can be pulled off. Work the faces in embroidery, washable fabric paint, or appliqué.

♡

When our girls were very young, I had just begun to try my hand at toymaking. I still marvel at how much they loved those limp, ugly little figures that I called toys. My children saw past the exteriors and into the heart of the matter.

♡

Now that our oldest daughter is married and starting her own family, I recall spanking her only once. After this seemingly necessary act, I went to my bedroom and cried because I hadn't wanted to spank her. Quietly, Kim slipped into my room, sat down beside me, and hugged me. "Please don't cry, Mama. I was bad and deserved a spanking," she consoled.

I don't think she was ever spanked again, for she hated to see me cry!

♡

Prior to motherhood, I was a nice person; I didn't use profanity or lose my temper or raise my voice. I was going to be "Mother Perfect," like the ones in the television programs. Those programs were our guides to how the perfect family lived. The fathers always wore suits; mothers wore aprons and were always cooking or cleaning, happily picking up after their broods. The children were always neat, not a hair out of place; their clothes were blindingly clean. The children never argued or fought with one another; they sat politely at the dinner table and carried on a meaningful conversation.

I don't know where or when I went wrong, but my waywardness seems to have been synchronized with the growth of our children!

♥

Older children let you know what they like. For toys, boys may prefer clowns in bright circus colors or fake fur animals. Girls might like pretty dolls to sit on their beds or babydolls to be "mommy" to. Girls usually like softer colors, such as pink or lavender. Soft toys for this age can be more whimsical or detailed in expression. Trims include buttons and pom-poms or anything you want to use. Soft toys for this age group can be made of felt but should not be overstuffed.

♥

What's in a name? Love. Each toy design, whether you're making one or hundreds, should be endowed with an identity. If the toy is not a surprise gift and the child is present during the making, let him be part of the naming process. My children love to study the new design and think of names that "suit the subject." Soft toys are more than inanimate objects to the little ones who will treasure them; they are childhood friends. We call our friends by their names, don't we?

♥

One of the sad things about these times is that we overdo; we forget what toys are created for. We are bombarded by the media, fads are created, and to keep up with the Joneses, we feel we must make sure our children aren't denied a particular toy. What often happens is that within five minutes of removing the persuasive packaging, the child discovers that the gimmickry was more interesting than the toy, which may have little or no real play value. Children aren't aware of the cost.

How many parents buy a costly toy for their child, only to reprimand him, "Take care of that. Do you know how much it cost?" Or they give a child a toy, but put it up out of reach so he can only look at it, and the parents admonish, "When you get older and can take care of things, then you can play with it." If the child is too young to play with the toy, don't give it to him; don't tell him about it. I hate the look-but-don't-touch attitude toward toys. Such items aren't toys; call them collectibles.

♥

For teenagers, "soft toys" are renamed "soft sculpture" and are used as decorations in their rooms rather than as items of play. Wacky expressions and weird, exaggerated shapes are fun for teens. Teenagers like reflections of their interests: boys, girls, phones, cars, etc. This is an age of fads and collections, like rainbows and unicorns.

♥

Large pillow silhouettes are fun. Leave them plain, relying on the texture of the fabric for the focal point, or get fancy with loads of trim and detail. These simple pillow shapes allow lots of room for your own creativity. (See pages 81-90.)

♥

Children grow up so fast, but I did not always think so. I recall when the girls, teens at the time, were having a food fight in our newly remodeled dining room. I walked in to calm the noise and found catsup and mashed potatoes on the walls and ceiling! At that moment, the question ran through my mind, "Will they ever grow up? Will I *live* to see the day? Will *they*?" It definitely was not funny at the time. But time has a way of consolidating those years of childhood into a collage of highlights we can laugh about.

I make toys even now for my own children, but *never* a toy that is made by our company. My children have grown up surrounded by toys that I have designed. Just plucking a toy off the shelf and giving it to them is—well, it's unthinkable, considering my line of work.

Each child is special. For each of my children, I design a one-of-a-kind toy *especially* for him. Each knows that it was made just for him, because each child is so special to me, and no one else will ever have a toy just like that one. My children always get something made by loving hands from their mama. No matter what their age, they will always be my children. Though the toys cease to be items of play, they remain symbols of my special love for each individual.

♡

By the time we think we've learned how to be a parent, our children are grown!

♡

In my opinion, raising teenagers is similar to childbirth. As birth approaches, the pain intensifies and becomes more frequent. Just when we think we can bear no more, it happens—the healthy cry of a newborn child. At that moment, all pain is forgotten; that precious miracle of life was worth it all and so much more. And so it is with teens. As they approach adulthood, they want to take charge of their destiny. They try our nerves and patience. Time seems to stand still. About the time we think we can stand no more, it happens, almost miraculously—a young adult steps out into the world. In this realization, all of the pain of trying times is forgotten. The years we spent in nurturing this child from infancy to adulthood seem only a moment in time.

We enter a new stage in life, always parent and child, but now friends as adults. Thank God.

♡

Too old for toys? NEVER! We never outgrow our need for love or expressions of love. Did you know that toys and dolls are among the leading collectibles the world over? I like soft toys and dolls that are unique in materials, craftsmanship, or originality. I enjoy making sock sculpture characters. These are soft toys, but not "play" toys. This type of doll is a collectible work of art, something to hand down to my children. Today is tomorrow's history.

♡

Some of my favorite toy designs are named for special people who have influenced my life. In naming the toys for them, it's as if I'm sharing that person with others who enjoy those toys.

One angel design is named Luci, for a special lady. She was a lunchroom attendant when I was in grade school, and she was my friend. As time passed, she retired, and I grew up and married, started a family, and moved 3,000 miles away. Yet we maintained our friendship, communicating regularly. The last time I saw her, she was very ill. It was then that I discovered that through the years, she had saved all of the things I had ever given her—pictures, letters, etc. She had lovingly arranged them in a collage on the wall of her study. Shortly after my visit with her, I received word that my friend Lucretia had passed away. The last gift I had sent her had accompanied her to the hospital.

When I designed an angel, no other name was considered. Lucretia was shortened to Luci, with a heart over the *i* as a symbol of love for my special angel.

22

Our happiness is multiplied by the happiness we have given to others.

♡

A special Christmas. Great-grandma Jump was a frail, sweet little lady who had seen many years come and go, but she never seemed to enjoy the holidays very much, for each year meant more gloves, hankies, or socks to add to the ones in her chest, still un-used from years past. I decided to make a beautiful rag doll designed especially for Grandma. As the time for opening presents arrived, I watched with anticipation as Grandpa handed her my present. I held my breath as she opened the box; a hush fell over the room, and all eyes were on Grandma. As she gently lifted the doll to her breast, one tear trickled down her cheek. She got up without a word, cradling the be-loved doll in her arms, took it upstairs, and placed it on her bed. That doll was a trea-sured possession for the rest of her days. A toy—who would have thought of giving Grandma a toy at her age? Why not?

♡

Toys are not created just for people between the ages of one and ten. Toys are for the enjoyment of the child within us, no matter our age. As we get older, we don't call it playing; we call it collecting.

♡

I have participated in one particular craft show for a number of years, mainly because it's local. It's near and dear to my heart. One particular family has had a booth close to ours for several years. Their child, who is probably in her twenties, was born with Down's syndrome. Each year I look forward to seeing these friends.

This year, at the close of the craft show, I handed Susan a small doll named "Li'l Luv." I said, "Here is a Li'l Luv just for you." She hugged the doll to her face and flashed that beautiful, happy smile at me. She loved the doll. Then she said, "The doll's name is Kay. I love Kay." That really touched me. I did so little, and she appreciated it so much. Her thank you was a greater gift than the doll I had given her. Sometimes it takes very little to brighten someone's day, but when we reach out, it's surprising how much brighter our own day becomes.

♡

Smile—make your face happy!
Smile—your face needs the exercise!
Smile—brighten someone's day!

♡

A girl whom I knew only casually in our church called, asking if she could show me some ties she was making. She was not an accomplished seamstress, so when she showed me her work and asked for my opinion, I looked her square in the eye and stat-ed, "Those are the most atrocious things I have ever seen!" She returned my gaze with a shocked stare of disbelief—and we have been best friends for sixteen years now.

The moral of the story: Care enough to be honest. Too many people say what they think we want to hear, and not what they really feel. It doesn't help us learn or improve. What if I had said, "Yes, those are lovely"? She might have invested her time and money in making more of those dreadful ties, only to be told by shop owners that her product wasn't marketable.

We all need someone who can be honest with us. We need to be able to accept constructive criticism. I might have been too blunt, but if you had seen those ties! I did help my friend learn basic sewing skills. She will not go down in history as a world-renowned seamstress, but that's okay, because, in my book, she's the world's greatest friend.

♡

Learn to laugh at your mistakes—it won't hurt so bad when others do.

♡

If you try, but do not succeed, you may have *failed*, but you are not a *failure*. A failure is one who never tries.

♡

Belief in oneself is important, but having others believe in us inspires and encourages success. Don't say, "I can't"; say, "I'll try."

♡

Use the talents you possess; the woods would be very silent if no birds sang except the best.

♡

The old rule that we get back what we give is especially true of love.

♡

Learn to do with what you've got and God will give you more to do with.

The Cute Fruits

Here's a delightful way to introduce Baby to soft toys. The small shapes are easy for little hands to grasp, and infants will love the bright colors. This is an easy project for the beginner. Shapes may be left plain, but if you enjoy embroidering, let your imagination run free. Experiment with stitches to create fun faces.

Babies and toddlers aren't the only fans of these personable toys—I love to put them in a fruit bowl on my table. Take a basket of fruit to someone who needs cheering up. For anyone past the toddler stage, these fruits can be made out of felt. Leave them plain, or get fancy with trim.

THE CUTE FRUITS

Materials

Apple Andy: 6″ X 12″ piece of red fabric
Leaf: 3-1/2″ X 6″ piece of green fabric
Face: black and white embroidery floss

Rosanna Banana: 8″ X 10″ piece of yellow fabric
Face: brown, black, and red embroidery floss

Orville Orange: 5″ X 12″ piece of orange fabric
Face: brown, red, and white embroidery floss

Percy Pear: 6″ X 10″ piece of light green fabric
Stem: 3″ X 3-1/2″ piece of brown fabric
Face: black, white, and red embroidery floss

Plum Precocious: 5″ X 10″ piece of blue or purple fabric
Leaf: 3-1/2″ X 6″ piece of green fabric
Face: black and white embroidery floss

Stuffing: small amount of polyester fiberfill for each toy

Pattern Pieces

(See pages 97-99.)
Cut:
APPLE ANDY: (2) from red fabric
*LEAF: (2) from green fabric
ORVILLE ORANGE: (2) from orange fabric
PERCY PEAR: (2) from pale green fabric
*STEM: (1) from brown fabric
ROSANNA BANANA: (2) from yellow fabric
PLUM PRECOCIOUS: (2) from blue fabric

*The leaf may be used on apple, orange, or pear. The stem may be used on pear or apple.

Directions

Lay out the material with wrong sides of fabric tobether.
Cut out all pattern pieces.
For *all* fruit, trace the faces onto the fabric before removing the pattern from the fabric. Slip tracing paper (dressmaker's carbon paper), right side down, between the pattern and the right side of one fruit section. Trace.

APPLE: Pin the two leaf sections right sides together, and stitch, leaving straight edge open. Trim the tip of the leaf, as shown, and then clip curves.

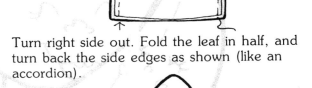

Turn right side out. Fold the leaf in half, and turn back the side edges as shown (like an accordion).

Pin the folded leaf on its side at the top of the apple. Tack.

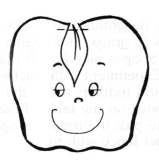

26

Pin the two APPLE sections with right sides together. Stitch, as shown, leaving open the space between dots.

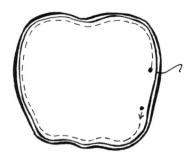

Clip curves, and turn right side out. Stuff smooth and firm. Turn under the raw edges of the opening, and stitch closed.

Work the face in whatever manner you choose or as I've diagramed on page 28.

♡

ORANGE: Pin the two ORANGE sections, right sides together. Stitch, leaving an opening as shown. Clip curves.

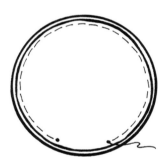

Turn right side out, and stuff firm and smooth. Close the seam. Work the face as suggested on page 28 or use your own idea.

♡

PEAR: Fold the stem in half lengthwise with right sides together. Stitch a narrow seam.

fold

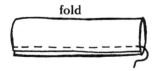

Turn the stem right side out, fold in half, and position the seam to the inside of the fold. Pin to the top of the pear as shown. Baste.

Pin the two sections of the PEAR with right sides together, and then stitch. Leave an opening as shown. Clip curves.

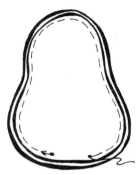

Turn the body right side out, and stuff it firm and smooth. Fold in the edges of the opening and slip-stitch them closed. The face may be embroidered as diagramed on page 28 or as you choose.

♡

BANANA: Pin the two sections of the banana, with right sides together, and stitch, leaving an opening as shown. Clip curves.

Turn the banana right side out. After stuffing it firm and smooth, close the opening. Work the face as diagramed on page 28 or as you choose.

♡

PLUM: Make the leaf as you would for the apple, and attach it in the same way. To make the body of the plum, follow the directions for assembling the apple. You may work the face as diagramed on page 28.

♡

Embroidery Instructions

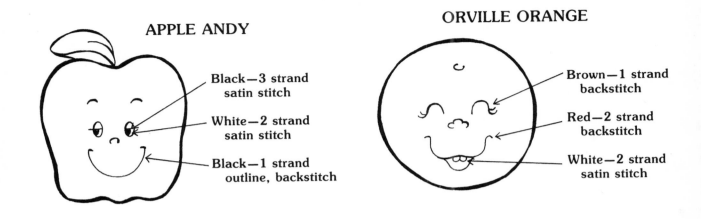

APPLE ANDY

Black—3 strand
satin stitch

White—2 strand
satin stitch

Black—1 strand
outline, backstitch

ORVILLE ORANGE

Brown—1 strand
backstitch

Red—2 strand
backstitch

White—2 strand
satin stitch

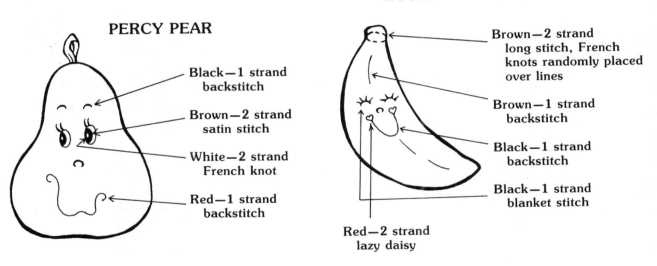

PERCY PEAR

Black—1 strand
backstitch

Brown—2 strand
satin stitch

White—2 strand
French knot

Red—1 strand
backstitch

ROSANNA BANANA

Brown—2 strand
long stitch, French
knots randomly placed
over lines

Brown—1 strand
backstitch

Black—1 strand
backstitch

Black—1 strand
blanket stitch

Red—2 strand
lazy daisy

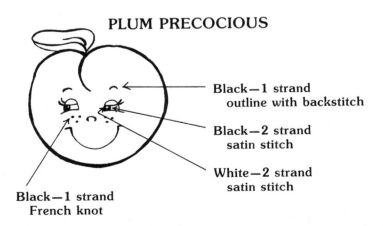

PLUM PRECOCIOUS

Black—1 strand
outline with backstitch

Black—2 strand
satin stitch

White—2 strand
satin stitch

Black—1 strand
French knot

These designs for facial features are suitable for any of the soft toys.

The Bo-Bear Family

   While their cottage in the woods is being remodeled, the Bo-Bears have come to the city for a little vacation. They are dressed in their Sunday best.
   Sugar Pops may growl every now and then, but he's really a softy at heart. Honey Pot cuddles the babies, Bobby and Bonny, wrapped in their blankets and snug as bugs in rugs.

MR. BO-BEAR (SUGAR POPS)

Materials

Body: 7″ X 37″ piece of brown brushed nylon tricot

Pants: 6″ X 10″ piece of plaid acrylic/wool blend

Jacket: 3-1/2″ X 14″ piece of colored felt

Necktie: enough 3/8″-wide ribbon to make a small bow at neck

Suspenders: cord or jute to tie from the top of the pants over the shoulder to the back of the pants

Face: 2 strands of black embroidery floss

Stuffing: small amount of polyester fiberfill

Pattern Pieces

(See pages 101–103.)

Cut:

BODY FRONT (2), BACK (1), ARMS (4), LEGS (4) from body fabric

JACKET FRONT (2), JACKET BACK (1) from felt

PANTS (2) from pants fabric

Directions

Cut out all pattern pieces.

ARMS & LEGS: Pin two leg pieces right

sides together, edges even. Stitch as shown; leave straight edge open.

Clip curves and use a narrow dowel to turn right side out. Repeat steps for other leg and arms.

BODY: Pin BODY FRONTS with right sides together and edges even. Stitch as shown. Clip curves.

Pin BODY FRONT to BACK, right sides together. Stitch; leave straight edge open. Clip curves.

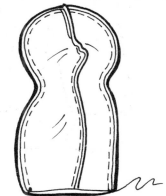

Turn right side out. Stuff arms, legs, and body to within 1/2″ of top.

Stuff to 1/2″ from top.

ASSEMBLY AND ATTACHMENT OF LIMBS: Turn in raw edge of body 1/4", baste FRONT and BACK together at bottom, and draw up slightly. (Top of leg should fit from side of body to center front seam.)

Turn in raw edges of arms and legs 1/4", baste top of each together, with seams at sides. Complete all legs and arms. Attach legs to the body with a blanket stitch or whipstitch.

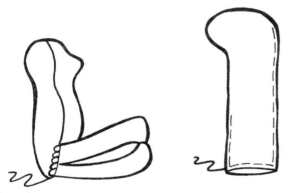

Attach arms to body side seams 1/4" below neck indention, using a blanket stitch.

EARS: Squeeze the corners of the head so that the stuffing is thinned. Start at the side as diagramed, stitch by hand through all thicknesses, and draw up thread tightly as shown.

FACE: Use two strands of black embroidery floss. NOSE is done in a satin stitch; MOUTH and EYES may be done in a straight stitch or as you wish.

CLOTHING: Pin pants, right sides together and edges even. Stitch FRONT and BACK center seams as shown.

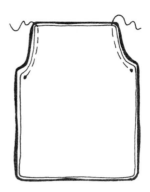

Fold pants, with right sides and center seams together; pin. Stitch the INNER LEG seam as shown. Clip at the crotch curve.

Turn right side out. Turn under 1/8" at waist and hemstitch or baste.

If the bottom of the pant leg was cut on the selvage or if you are using felt, there is no need to hem. You may pink the bottom of the pant legs OR turn them under 1/8" to hem or edge-stitch.

Pin JACKET FRONT to BACK, with shoulder and side seams even. Stitch shoulder seams and side seams. Turn stitching to wrong side.

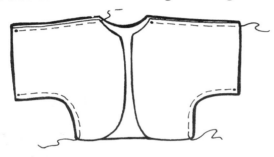

Put the pants on Papa Bear. Use cord or yarn to make the SUSPENDERS. Tie a knot in one end of the cord, tack to pants, as shown, take cord over the right shoulder, tie a knot at the back of the pant waist, and tack in place.

Put on his JACKET, and tie a small BOW around his neck.

MRS. BO-BEAR (HONEY-POT)

Materials
Body: 7" X 37" piece of brown brushed nylon tricot
Dress: 7" X 16" piece of bold print knit, or felt (easier to work with in a nonraveling fabric)
Apron: 3" X 4" piece of felt
Apron ties: 18" length of 3/8"-wide ribbon
Apron trim: 9" piece of narrow rickrack
Face: black embroidery floss
Stuffing: small amount of polyester fiberfill
Tiny fabric flowers for head, optional

Pattern Pieces
(See pages 101–103.)
Cut:
BODY FRONT (2), BACK (1), ARMS (4), LEGS (4) from body fabric
DRESS (2) from bold print or lightweight felt
APRON (1) from felt

Directions
Cut out all pattern pieces.
ARMS & LEGS: Pin two leg pieces right sides together, edges even. Stitch as shown; leave straight edge open.

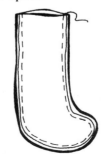

Clip curves and use a narrow dowel to turn right side out. Repeat steps for other leg and arms.

BODY: Pin BODY FRONTS with right sides together and edges even. Stitch as shown. Clip curves.

Pin BODY FRONT to BACK, right sides together. Stitch; leave straight edge open. Clip curves.

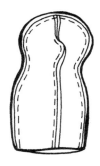

Turn right side out. Stuff arms, legs, and body to within 1/2" from top.

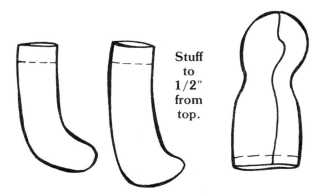

Stuff to 1/2" from top.

ASSEMBLY AND ATTACHMENT OF LIMBS: Turn in raw edge of body 1/4", baste FRONT and BACK together at bottom, and draw up slightly. (Top of leg should fit from side of body to center front seam.)

Turn in raw edges of arms and legs 1/4", baste top of each together, with seams at sides. Complete all legs and arms. Attach legs to the body with a blanket stitch or whipstitch.

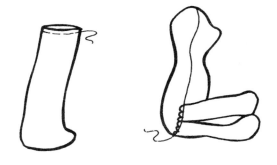

Attach arms to body side seams 1/4" below neck indention, using a blanket stitch.

EARS: Squeeze the corners of the head so that the stuffing is thinned. Start at the side as diagramed, stitch by hand through all thicknesses, and draw up thread tightly as shown.

FACE: Use two strands of black embroidery floss. NOSE is done in a satin stitch; EYES are in French knots, MOUTH in a straight stitch or as you wish.

CLOTHING: Stitch narrow rickrack around outer curved edge of APRON as shown.

For APRON TIES, fold ribbon in half to find the center, then fold apron in half to find its center. Place the center of the ribbon on the apron center and pin the top edges of ribbon and apron even. Stitch.

Slit center back of the DRESS from the neck edge down 1-1/2". Pin BACK to FRONT, right sides together with edges even. Stitch shoulder seams.

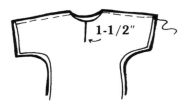

Turn under 1/8" along sleeve edge, then edge-stitch.

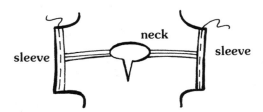

Fold dress pieces together again, pin, and stitch side seams. Clip curves under ARMS.

Turn right side out. Turn under NECK edge 1/8" and edge-stitch. Sew a snap to top of BACK NECK edges.

If the dress was made of nonraveling fabric, there is no need to hem, but if you wish, turn under 1/4" and hem.

Optional: Stitch small fabric FLOWERS above one ear, as shown.

THE TWINS (BOBBY AND BONNY)

Materials
Bodies: two 5″ X 10″ pieces of brown
    brushed nylon tricot
Blankets: two 5-1/2″ squares of felt or fabric
Faces: black embroidery floss
Bows: enough ribbon up to 3/8″ wide to tie
    around neck of each baby (one pink bow,
    one blue)
Stuffing: small amount of polyester fiberfill

Pattern Pieces
(See page 101.)
Cut:
BODY (2) from body fabric (for each)
BLANKET (1) from blanket fabric (for each)

Directions
Cut out all pattern pieces.
BODY: Pin two body pieces right sides
together, with edges even. Stitch as shown
and leave open between dots. Clip curves.

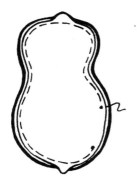

Turn, stuff softly, and slip stitch the opening
closed.

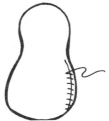

EARS: Squeeze top corners of the head to
thin stuffing in ear area. Stitch through all
thicknesses from the dot at the side of the
head to the dot at the top, as shown. Pull up
the thread tightly to gather the ear, and knot
securely. Repeat for other ear.

FACE: Use two strands of black embroidery
floss to work features as shown.

Place the baby on a blanket square, fold up
the bottom, fold right side to left, then left
over right, turning under the raw edges.
Blindstitch the blanket in place. Tie a pink
bow around the neck and blanket of one
baby, and tie a blue bow around the neck
and blanket of the other baby.

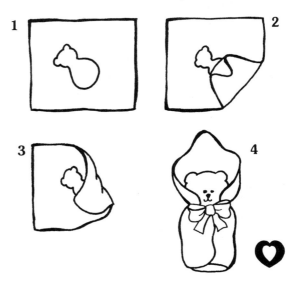

Bear in mind these bright ideas
for the soft toys you make . . .

- Decorate curtains or the bottoms of window shades with unstuffed versions of the soft toys or pillow pals. Larger stuffed toys of the same design placed on a child's bed will provide a coordinated decor which both you and your child will enjoy.

- The Bo-Bear Family will make the perfect gift for a young child in a family with a new baby. He or she will have his own babies to care for with the twins, Bobby and Bonny.

- Your "spacey" friends will surely appreciate your humor in a gift of the rocket ship and crew. Name a crew member for the recipient by appliquéing his or her name on the toy.

- Even preschoolers can enjoy the thrill of making and decorating some of the simple pillow pal designs and giving them to friends and grandparents. What a super reversal—the child gives the grandparents a toy to love!

- Wall hangings of pillow pal shapes are easy to make. Select a background fabric that is heavy enough to hang smoothly or back your fabric with quilting or a material of similar weight. Make loops from tubes of fabric and stitch both ends of each loop to the top of your hanging. Create a border with ribbon, blanket binding, bias tape, or cording.

    Your design will have added interest if you attach fiberfill to the back of it and stitch along detail lines to create a trapunto effect. After you've completed your design, attach it to the hanging.

    Use a curtain rod or dowel to suspend your wall decoration.

- Though they're "in-season" year-round, Bunny & Carrot and Bell-Ve-Deer are especially ideal gifts at Easter and Christmas.

- Attach small pieces of Velcro fastener to the webbed hands and feet of the long-legged frogs so that they can hang around the bedpost or even your neck.

- Use the Skinny Minnie pattern to create a "Queen of Hearts" for your next bridge party. You can add many a heart to her face and costume.

- When making soft toys for teens, use fabrics with the young people's school colors in them. These collectibles can be special hits with college students away from home.

- For a housewarming gift, give a friend an apple or orange tree. Make up several of the fruit of your choice and hang them on a graceful branch you've set in a container of tightly-packed sand or small pebbles. Wrap the container in burlap to simulate a tree ready for planting and add a tag identifying the variety of fruit, such as "Friendship Apple."

- Place a bowl or basket of fruit on your dining table for a touch of color. For a sick friend, remember that "an apple a day keeps the doctor away." Just think what a basket of several cute fruits can do!

- The cute fruits can be assembled into a lightweight mobile sure to entertain anyone, especially those confined to bed or a wheelchair.

- A school of sea creatures will add whimsy to any room of a beach house.

- Terri Mouse and Fergus the Frog will make interesting paperweights for your favorite office workers.

Rocket Ship & Crew

Blast off to outer space with friendly, far-out aliens who are easy to make and hard to beat—if you're a space-crazed kid in search of cheap thrills. Stitched on the outside, the toys in this group present a lot of creative opportunities for playing with color and trims. Felt is recommended for these designs, because there's no raveling and felt has no wrong side, so pattern pieces can be cut in any direction.

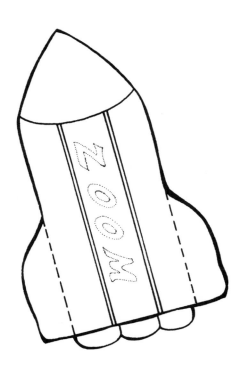

ROCKET SHIP

Materials
Ship: 12″ X 16″ piece of white felt
Cone: red felt scrap
Thrusters: grey felt scraps
Letters: blue felt scraps
Stripes: 19″ length of trim such as rickrack or
   braid
Stuffing: polyester fiberfill

Pattern Pieces
(See pages 105—107.)
Cut:
SHIP (2) from white felt
CONE (1), THRUSTERS (6), LETTERS (3)
   from assorted colors of felt scraps
STRIPES (2) from any kind of trim

Directions
Cut out all pattern pieces.
Pin the stripes on the ROCKET section, extending them at the top past the seam line of the rocket's CONE (the cone will cover the raw edge of the trim). Extend the trim at the bottom by 1/2″, and then fold it under and tack it.

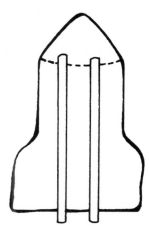

Pin the CONE to the top of the ROCKET front, align the top edges, and stitch as shown.

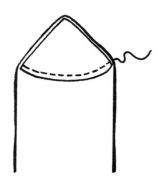

Pin the pairs of THRUSTERS together, keeping the edges even. Stitch as shown, leaving the straight edges open. Baste the thrusters together in a row—sides touching—along their straight edges.

Pin the THRUSTERS to the back of the rocket's FRONT (see next page). Baste the unit just inside the seam line of the ROCKET.

38

Pin the BACK to the FRONT of the rocket, keeping the edges even. Stitch as shown, but leave an opening to add stuffing. Stitch straight lines from the rocket's sides to the thrusters to form FINS (see illustration).

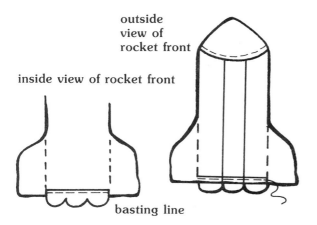

inside view of rocket front

outside view of rocket front

basting line

Stuff softly. Machine-stitch the opening closed. Glue LETTERS on the rocket as shown.

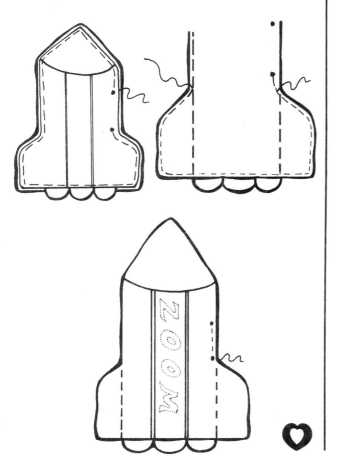

ZORK

Materials
Body: 11" X 12" piece of orange felt
Hair: yellow felt scrap
Toenails: pink felt scraps
Eyes: white and black felt scraps
Cheeks: red felt scraps
Nose: green felt scraps
Mouth: black embroidery floss
Stuffing: small amount of polyester fiberfill

Pattern Pieces
(See page 109.)
Cut:
BODY (2) from felt
TOENAILS (6), CHEEKS (2), NOSE (1),
EYES (4), HAIR (2) from scraps of felt

Directions
Cut out all pattern pieces.
Pin the two BODY sections together, keeping the edges even. Insert HAIR between HEAD sections (as shown), and pin it. Stitch a narrow seam, leaving an opening to stuff.

39

Stuff softly. If a machine was used to do the previous stitching, machine-stitch the opening closed.

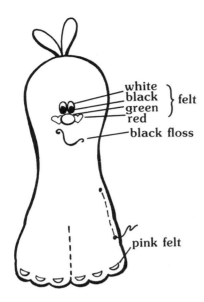

Glue the FACE and the TOENAILS as diagramed. Outline-stitch the MOUTH, using one strand of black embroidery floss.

Zork says:
To handle yourself, use your head.
To handle others, use your heart.

MEECH

Materials
Body fabric: 8″ X 18″ piece of yellow felt
Hair: blue felt scraps
Nose: orange felt scraps
Eyes: black felt scraps
Toenails: pink felt scraps
Mouth & ankles: black embroidery floss
Stuffing: polyester fiberfill

Pattern Pieces
(See page 111.)
Cut:
BODY (2) from felt
HAIR (1), NOSE (1), EYES (2), TOENAILS (2), from assorted colors of felt

Directions
Cut out all pattern pieces.
Pin the two BODY sections together, keeping the edges even. Insert hair (the seam line of the hair will be inside the stitch line of the topknot), and pin. Stitch a 1/8″ seam around the outer edge, and leave an opening as shown.

Stuff softly. Stitch the opening closed by machine. Glue EYES, NOSE, and TOE-NAILS as diagramed. Outline-stitch MOUTH and ANKLES, using one strand of black embroidery floss.

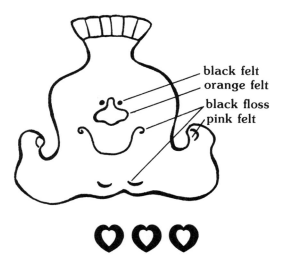

black felt
orange felt
black floss
pink felt

Meech says:
People are usually as happy as they make up their minds to be.

ZIRD

Materials
Body: white felt scrap
Tail & feather: red felt scrap
Foot & feather: orange felt scrap
Wing: gray felt scrap
Beak: yellow felt scrap
Eyes, toenails, & feather: blue felt scraps
Mouth & nose: black embroidery floss
Stuffing: small amount of polyester fiberfill

Pattern Pieces
(See page 113.)
Cut:
BODY (2), FOOT (2), BEAK (1), TAIL (1), FEATHERS (2 small and 1 large), WING (1), EYES (2), TOENAILS (3), from assorted colors of felt scraps

Directions
Cut out all pattern pieces.
Pin the two BODY sections together, keeping the edges even. Insert TAIL FEATHERS (stitch line of tail inside stitch line of body), and pin. Place the two smaller feathers over the larger feather, as shown. Insert these between BODY sections, and pin.

feathers

foot

Pin the two FEET together, with the edges even, and stitch a 1/8″ seam around the outer edge of the foot. Leave the straight edge open. Insert the straight edge of the foot between BODY sections (stitch line of foot just inside stitch line of body), and pin. Stitch the BODY, using a 1/8″ seam. Leave an opening.

Stuff softly. Stitch the opening closed by machine. Glue WING, BEAK, EYES, and TOENAILS as diagramed. Outline-stitch the MOUTH and add a French knot for the NOS-TRIL, using one strand of black embroidery floss.

MICRO GROTS

Materials
Body: yellow felt scrap
Face & toenails: black embroidery floss
Heart: red embroidery floss
Stuffing: small amount of polyester fiberfill

Pattern Pieces
(See page 113.)
Cut:
BODY (2) from felt

Directions
Pin the two BODY sections together with the edges even. Stitch, leaving an opening as shown.

Stuff softly. Machine-stitch the opening closed.
FACE: Use one strand of black embroidery floss to outline-stitch the mouth. Use French knots for the EYES, and straight stitches for the TOES. For the HEART, do two lazy daisy stitches, using two strands of red embroidery floss.

enlarged to show lazy daisy stitch

Sea Creatures

In this grouping of simple-to-make toys, there's something for everyone. Study Oggie and Aggie Octopi, taking note of how you can vary a single toy design by changing fabric and trim. One version is suitable for infants, while the other is appealing to grown-up children. You'll enjoy making Star-la Fish, Golda Fish, and Caesar the Sea Horse— all of felt and fun to trim. Suggested fabrics for other designs in this section range from cotton to acrylic pile (fake fur), and sizes vary.

GOLDA FISH

You'll fall hook, line, and sinker for Golda. She's easy to make from any color of felt—a great way to use the small scraps. This is a versatile design. String Golda on a line attached to a stick for a fishing pole. Little boys love that. String several to make a mobile. Decorate her for use as an ornament or a pin cushion. And if, like me, you hate to clean the fish tank, but want fish, here's an idea. Drain the water from the fish tank, decorate with fake greenery or colorful rocks, and stock it with several Goldas. You can enjoy an attractive fish tank without the usual mess.

Materials

Body: scraps in assorted colors of felt
Eyes: two small movable eyes from hobby
   shop (or two small circles of felt, tiny buttons, or embroidery)
Stuffing: polyester fiberfill

Pattern Pieces

(See page 121.)
Cut:
BODY (2), TOP FIN (1), BOTTOM FIN (2),
   BOTTOM of BODY (1) from felt

Directions

Cut out all pattern pieces.
Stitch on the outside, close to edge. Pin the two BODY sections together, and insert the TOP FIN between the BODY sections. Stitch,

as shown. Stop at the bottom base of the TAIL, as indicated below.

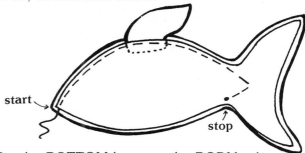

Pin the BOTTOM between the BODY sides, keeping all edges even, (see following illustration: one point at center of front seam, one point at center of tail). Insert the BOTTOM FINS between the BOTTOM and SIDES, evenly on each side, and pin in place. Start stitching at the center back of the TAIL, folding back the top half of the TAIL so as not to catch it in the stitching. Stitch to the NOSE, catching the FIN in the seam.

Turn and continue stitching just past the FIN. Leave an opening, as shown, to stuff.

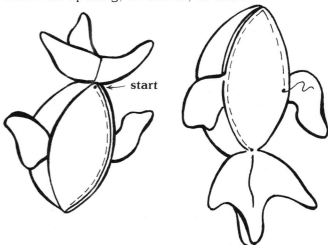

Stuff softly. Machine-stitch the opening closed. Glue on movable eyes as shown.

44

STAR-LA FISH

"Dahling, stars aren't born, they are made." This one is easily sewn from felt, and she's fun to dress, so get out the feathers, sequins, and any other gaudy trim. She's the Miss Piggy of Ocean Boulevard. This design is for teens and alleged adults.

Materials

Body: two 9" X 12" pieces of light-colored felt
Stuffing: polyester fiberfill
Face: scraps of felt and black embroidery floss
Outfit: Make this star shine any way you wish. For trim, you could use felt, lace, nylon net, silk flowers, old jewelry, or feathers.

Pattern Pieces

(See page 123.)
Cut:
BODY (2) from felt
EYELIDS (2), MOUTH (1) from scraps of felt
SAND DOLLARS (2) from scrap of white felt

Directions

Pin BODY sections together, keeping all edges even. Stitch, as shown, with a 1/8" seam allowance. Leave open between dots to stuff. Here's a hint to simplify stuffing: After stitching one side of an arm, a leg, or the head, push a "strand" of stuffing between felt sections before turning the curve to stitch the other side. That way, you've already got some stuffing into those hard-to-reach areas, and it's easier to finish stuffing.

Stuff softly. If the previous stitching was done by machine, machine-stitch the opening closed.

To finish, position the facial features, and glue or stitch them in place (embroider if you wish). Glue or stitch silk flowers on the head, and dress Star-la with scraps of lace or net. Use felt sand dollars for the bodice.

Star-la says:
You can't sit on the bank and fish for friends. You must get in the water and swim with them.

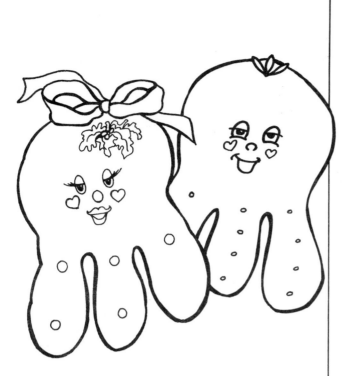

Turn right side out (a small dowel is helpful for turning and for pushing stuffing into hard-to-reach areas). Stuff. Turn in the raw edges of the opening, and close by whip-stitching.

OGGIE OCTOPI & AGGIE

This is a simple flatsy design with baby in mind. It's made of cotton fabric and has embroidered features. However, this same pattern (as Miss Aggie) can get a completely new look when made of acrylic pile and trimmed with felt scraps, silk flowers, and a bow (not for small children). Oggie's directions are for the infant toy version.

Materials
Body: 10″ X 18″ piece of cotton fabric
Features: black and pink embroidery floss
Stuffing: polyester fiberfill

Pattern Pieces
(See page 117.)
Cut:
BODY (2) from cotton fabric

Directions
Cut out all pattern pieces.
Pin BODY sections, with right sides together and all edges aligned. Stitch, as shown, leaving an opening for turning and stuffing. Clip curves. Reinforce curves and stress points by stitching them twice.

Embroider rows of French knots on the tentacles, using six strands of black embroidery floss. To make the facial lines, outline-stitch, using two strands of black embroidery floss. Using two strands of pink embroidery floss, add some color to the cheeks with a couple of lazy daisy stitches. Satin-stitch the eyes, using four strands of black embroidery floss.

MISS AGGIE

This variation is made with acrylic pile, commonly called fake fur (remember to cut the nap down). Follow the directions given for Oggie for stitching, stuffing, and closing. Facial features are cut from scraps of felt. The circles on the tentacles are of terry cloth (plastic soles from children's sleepers, cut into circles, can likewise add texture). If Miss Aggie will be used as a toy for a very young child, her features should be stitched in place. Otherwise, it's okay to glue the features to the face. The bow and silk flowers are stitched on.

CLAMITY JANE

Clamity looks best in fabrics with nap, such as velvet, velveteen, and corduroy, but she can be made from other fabrics. You may want to add some polystyrene pellets (the "beans" used in bean bag chairs) to the shell stuffing. The finished size is about 5-1/2" across. Clamity can be used as a pin cushion or jewelry box.

Materials
Shell: 7" X 14" piece of white velveteen
Lining: 7" X 14" piece of aqua fabric
Face: scrap of beige fabric and some black
    embroidery floss
Pearl: one 1/2" white pom-pom
Stuffing: small amount of quilt batting and/or
    polyester fiberfill
Bow (optional): 1 foot of 1/2"-wide ribbon

Pattern Pieces
(See page 119.)
Cut:
SHELL (2) from white velveteen
SHELL LINING (2) from aqua cotton fabric
FACE (1) from beige cotton fabric

Directions
Cut out all pattern pieces.
If you wish to trace scallop lines and facial features, do so before removing the pattern from the fabric.

To give SHELLS the trapunto treatment, pin the batting to the wrong side of one shell. With the shell right-side-up, stitch (by hand or machine) from the center back, as shown. Trim away excess batting from around the edge of the shell. Repeat the steps for the other shell.

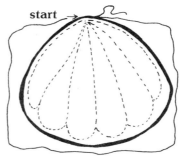

Pin the SHELL'S LINING (cotton fabric) to the SHELL with right sides together, keeping the edges even. Stitch as shown, leaving an opening between the dots on the side. Clip curves. Turn and add *only* enough stuffing (or styrene pellets) to give shape. Turn in the raw edges of the opening, and whipstitch them closed. Repeat these steps for the other SHELL.

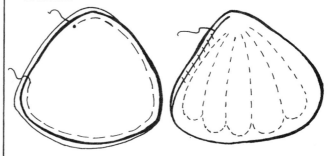

To make the FACE, pin the wrong side of the fabric to a layer of batting. Work the FACE with two strands of black embroidery floss. The eyes are French knots, and the MOUTH is done in backstitching. Take one small stitch at the NOSE (pearl) to indent.

Trim batting to 3/8" inside of outer edge (just inside baste line).

Run a baste line 1/4″ from the outer edge of the FACE, drawing up the thread just enough to be able to turn the raw edges under (you may wish to add a little more stuffing before positioning on shell). Pin in place, and then blindstitch the FACE to the SHELL, making sure raw edges are turned under as you stitch.

Place the LINING sides of both SHELLS together, with the edges even. Whipstitch backs of SHELLS securely together. Stitch a bow at the hinge, where the backs were stitched together. Glue a white pom-pom at the NOSE indention.

♡ ♥ ♡

CAESAR THE SEA HORSE

He's "sew" simple to make and such fun to decorate. You may want to leave him plain, with only the eye as decoration, or add lots of embroidery, or cover him with sequins for an eye-catching ornament. Caesar can also be used as a pin cushion.

Materials
Body: 10″ X 10″ piece of yellow felt
Eye: scraps of felt in three colors, black embroidery floss
Stuffing: small amount of polyester fiberfill
Trim: (optional) Add any kind of trim and as much or as little as you wish.

Pattern Pieces
(See page 115.)
Cut:
BODY (2) from yellow felt
EYE from scraps of felt

Directions
Cut out all pattern pieces.
Felt has no wrong side, and stitching is done on the outside.
Pin the BODY sections together, with all edges even. Match the thread to the color of felt for a more professional finish. Stitch around the outer edge, but leave the space between the dots open in order to stuff. Put polyester fiberfill between the layers of felt in the HEAD and TAIL areas before stitching closed, as these hard-to-reach areas are difficult to stuff after being stitched.

Stuff softly. If the earlier stitching was done by machine, close the opening with the same length of machine stitching. Decorate as you wish.

♡ ♥ ♡

Caesar says:
 Stuff softly and carry a big stitch.

Lovable Huggables

This assortment of soft toys includes a cotton puppy and bunny, a terry cloth mouse and reindeer, three frogs, Skinny Minnie in her many guises, a furry rabbit with a carrot-carrying pouch, and a couple of clowns resplendent in big top costumes. These designs range from simple to advanced. The toys in this section make especially nice gifts, and the patterns lend themselves to endless variations so that you needn't duplicate any design exactly, unless you want to do so.

PUPPY LUV

This design is for tiny tots. Cotton fabric, polyester fiberfill stuffing, and embroidered features are recommended. The tail and also the pouch that holds an object have been eliminated on this design to make it safe for infants. For a child past infant stage, you may want to add a pouch like that used with Bunny & Carrot on page 65. Use that pouch pattern on this design and attach it as directed for Bunny & Carrot.

Materials
Body: 11″ X 18″ piece of cotton fabric
Ear lining: scrap of lining fabric
Face: Black and pink embroidery floss
Decoration: 24″ length of 1/2″-wide ribbon
Stuffing: polyester fiberfill

Pattern Pieces
(See pages 135-137.)
Cut:
BODY (2), EARS (2) from body fabric
EAR LINING (2) from lining fabric

Directions
Cut out all pattern pieces.

Pin the two BODY sections, with right sides together and all edges even. Stitch, as shown, leaving open between the dots in order to turn and stuff.
Clip curves.

Turn right side out. Stuff. Turn in the raw edges of the opening, and then whipstitch closed.

bottom view

Use crochet thread to make tie tacks at the base of the ARMS and LEGS, as shown.

50

For the FACE, embroider the EYES and NOSE with a satin stitch. Use three strands of black embroidery floss. To make the MOUTH LINE, backstitch with one strand of black embroidery floss. Freckles are French knots. The TONGUE and BELLY BUTTON are done by satin-stitching with three strands of pink embroidery floss.

Pin one EAR LINING to one EAR, keeping right sides together, and all edges even. Stitch as shown, and leave the straight edge open for turning. Repeat for the other ear. Turn right side out, and turn in the raw edges. Baste the edges together, and draw up the basting stitches to gather the top of the EAR. After carefully placing the ears, pin them in the desired positions. Whipstitch securely to the HEAD. You're finished, except for tying a bow around Puppy Luv's neck and giving him a hug.

TERRI MOUSE

For this design, I like to use fabrics with nap, such as terry cloth, corduroy, or acrylic pile (fake fur). Make Terri out of white fabric, and sew a sprig of holly and berries (artificial) over one ear, or tie a small bow at the end of the tail to make a cute stocking stuffer.

Materials
Body: 4 ″ X 20″ piece of terry cloth
Ears: scrap of felt
Tail: 9″ of macramé cord (rat tail) *
Movable eyes
Stuffing: small amount of polyester fiberfill
Optional: Whiskers can be made of black embroidery floss.

*Tail can be made from shoe string or ribbon.

Pattern Pieces
(See page 127.)
Cut:
BODY SIDE (2), BODY BOTTOM (1), from body fabric
EARS (2) from felt

Directions
Cut out all pattern pieces.

Cut fabrics with nap in direction of arrows.

Baste one end of the TAIL at the large dot, as shown, right side up on one BODY SIDE. Pin the BODY with right sides together and the edges even, stitch the center back seam between the dots, backstitching at start and finish.

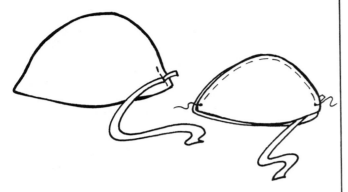

With right sides together, match the notches of the body and bottom sections, and pin or baste. Push the tail into the back section while sewing the body to the bottom. With the bottom side down, stitch, leaving an opening between the dots at the side, in order to turn and stuff. Slip-stitch to close the seam.

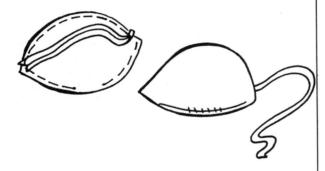

The pattern shows the placement of the ears. Pin the EAR in the desired position, gently curving the ear. Whipstitch in place (it may be glued if you prefer).

Small movable eyes and a 1/4″ pom-pom for the NOSE were glued in place as finishing touches.

Whiskers are made by using six strands of black embroidery floss. Tie a double knot 2″ from the end, as shown. Insert a needle into the whisker area, and come across and out the other side. Tie the knot close to the surface, and trim whiskers even with the other side.

To stiffen the WHISKERS, separate the strands, and with a drop of glue (white, clear-drying) between your thumb and forefinger, pull the strands through the glue on your fingers. Make sure the strands are separated as they dry.

Terri Mouse says:
Criticize a child in whispers, but praise him out loud.

BELL-VE-DEER

This fellow has been a favorite holiday character at our house for years. I like to see a sprig of holly in his hair or a redbird perched on his antlers. After Christmas, you needn't put him away; he's sure to delight the little ones all year long.

Materials

Body: one pair of white terry-lined, narrow-band cotton work socks
Ear lining: Scrap of cotton print fabric
Antlers: 6″ X 16″ piece of white fabric
Hair: 84″ length of white yarn
Yarn decorative ties: six strands of yarn, in Christmas colors, tied around wrists, ankles, and neck
Face: a red 1″ pom-pom, black felt scrap, red embroidery floss
Stuffing: polyester fiberfill
Decoration (optional): small redbird from hobby shop or florist, or a sprig of holly (plastic or silk) to place between the antlers

Pattern Pieces

(See page 141.)
Cut:
BODY (1), SNOUT (1), TAIL (1), ARMS (2), EARS (2), from sock*
EAR LINING (2) from lining fabric
ANTLERS (2) from antler fabric (white/beige)

*For interesting texture, some types of socks are best used wrong side out.

Cutting diagram

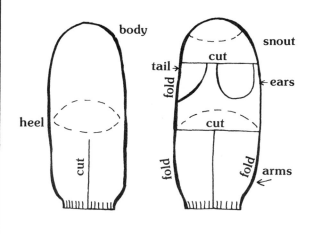

Directions

Cut out all pattern pieces.

To make the LEGS, use one sock, right side out. Lay the sock flat, with the heel faceup. From the center and 1/2″ below the heel, draw a straight line to the bottom of the sock. Using a 1/4″ seam, stitch as shown, leaving a 2″ opening on one inner leg for turning and stuffing. Clip the curve. Turn right side out, stuff smoothly, and blindstitch the opening closed.

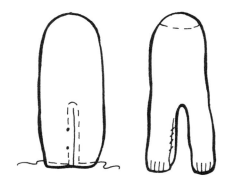

To make the ARMS, fold one arm right sides together lengthwise of sock. Stitch down the side and across the banded end as shown, leaving the top open. Turn and stuff the ARM to within 1/2″ of the top. Repeat these steps for the other arm.

The elastic banding will serve as the hand portion of the arm. Turn in raw edge 1/2″, and baste. Position the arms evenly on the body's sides and whipstitch securely in place.

Stuff the SNOUT, turn under about 1/2″ of the raw edge. Baste. Position on the face, and center the top of the snout about 1″ below the stitching on the toe or about 3″ below the top of the head. *Note that the toe stitch of the SNOUT serves as the MOUTH, and be sure the stitching is on the bottom half of the snout for a smile. Pin the snout in the desired position, and stitch it to the face.

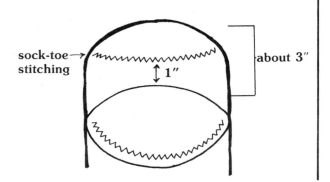

Fold the TAIL right sides together, and stitch the curved edge as shown. Leave the straight edge open. Turn and stuff softly. Turn in the raw edge (1/2″) and baste. Position the tail at the low center back—at the sock's heel— and stitch securely in place.

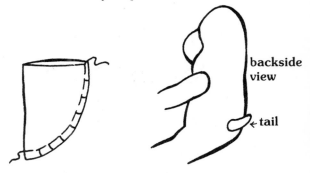

Pin the ANTLERS with right sides together and edges even. Stitch as shown, leaving the straight edge open. Clip curves. Turn right side out, and stuff smoothly (a knitting needle is helpful to push stuffing into hard-to-reach areas). Turn in the raw edges (1/2″) and baste. Position at the center top of the HEAD. Stitch securely in place.

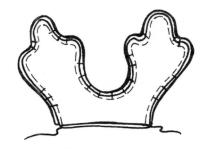

Pin the EAR LINING to the EAR, with right sides together and edges even. Stitch the curved edge as shown, leaving the straight edge open. Clip the curve. Turn right side

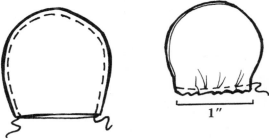

out. Fold raw edges in (1/4″), baste the edges together, and draw up the basting stitch at the bottom of the ear to measure about 1″, then knot it. Repeat for the other ear.

Position the ear with the ear lining facing forward at the side of the antlers, then whipstitch securely.

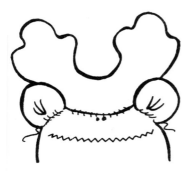

To make HAIR, you'll need 20 strands of 3"-long yarn (wind 20 loops of yarn around a piece of 3"-wide cardboard). Cut the ends, and use a 5" length of yarn to tie tightly in the middle to form a "fluff" of hair.
Stitch the center of the hair at the center-front base of the antlers.

For decorative ties, use six strands of yarn, all one color or a mix, tie snugly around ARM/wrist and LEG/ankle, where ribbing ends and sock begins. Knot twice and leave yarn ends about 2" in length. Tie yarn snugly under snout, above arms to form NECK. Knot twice, tie a bow with yarn and cut the ends of yarn to measure 2".

To add a NOSE, glue a red 1" pom-pom in position, top center front of the snout. Glue the EYES at the base of the SNOUT, spacing them evenly on either side of the NOSE. To make the MOUTH, first study the FACE; you might want to measure and place pins an equal distance from each side of the NOSE. Using six strands of red embroidery floss, define the MOUTH by long straight stitches which run directly above the toe-stitching of the sock, as shown. We used "smile" lines at the corner of the mouth.

GLOVEY, DEAR

Make "Glovey" by simply stuffing an old glove (no cutting!). Whipstitch the bottom of the glove closed. To make ANTLERS, loop the thread around the base of two fingers, draw up tightly, and knot twice. Repeat this step for the other antler. Cut two felt ears and two felt ear linings. Place the ear linings on the ears, with the straight edges even, fold each base together, and stitch to the base of each antler. Form the snout by folding the thumb over to touch the thumb's base, and blindstitch in place. To make the legs, take one long stitch from back to front, looping around the bottom of the glove, to where the stitch began, then draw up the stitch snugly and knot twice. For the FACE, glue on movable eyes and a 1/4" pom-pom nose, then embroider a smile. Tie a ribbon, with a spare ornament, snugly under snout for a NECK. See the photo in the Family Album.

THE LONG-LEGGED FROG

This bean bag toy is great for older children. It was one of our daughter's favorite dragga-ble, drapable toys. He is stuffed with a mix of polystyrene beads and polyester fiberfill, which makes him light and squishy. (Add aquarium gravel to the stuffing if you want more weight.) His body, hands, and feet are constructed of felt, but the arms and legs are cotton fabric. Try a bright or bold print, but avoid lightweight fabrics that are sheer or stiff.

Materials

Body & feet: 9″ X 12″ piece of green felt
Face & hands: 9″ X 12″ piece of white felt
Legs & arms: 1/3 yard of print fabric
Eyes: two white 1″ pom-poms and two black 1/2″ pom-poms
Nose: black floss
Bow: 12″ length of ribbon
Stuffing: polyester fiberfill and polystyrene beads (aquarium gravel, optional)

Pattern Pieces

(See page 129-131.)
Cut:
BODY (2), FEET (4) from body color felt
FACE (1), HANDS (4) from white felt
LEGS (2), ARMS (2) from print fabric

Directions

Cut out all pattern pieces.

To make the BODY front, position the FACE on one BODY section, with the top edges even, and topstitch along the mouth line of the FACE, using red thread.

For the NOSE, make two French knots, using six strands of black floss. (See the illustration.) To make the ARMS and LEGS, fold an ARM in half lengthwise, with right sides together. Stitch, leaving both ends open. Turn the ARM right side out. Repeat these steps for the other ARM and the LEGS.

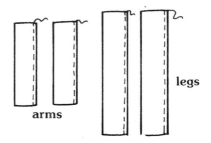

Now you can attach the HANDS to the ARMS.
Layer two HANDS, keeping the edges even. Pin them at the bottom. Sandwich the lower ARM between the two layers. Position the ARM seam to the center back of the HAND, and pin. Topstitch all around the outer edge of the HAND.

Repeat these steps for attaching the other ARM and the LEGS.

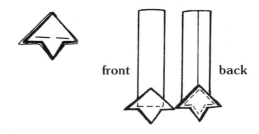

Stuff the ARMS and LEGS softly to within an inch of the top.

Position the ARM and LEG seams to the center back. Baste raw edges together 1/2" from the top.

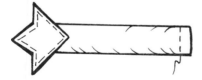

In assembling the BODY, follow these steps. Place the body front, faceup on the body back, keeping all edges even. Pin at the top. Sandwich the top of the ARM between the body front and back. (The arm seam will be to the back of the body, and the baste line of the arm will be inside the stitch line of the body.) Baste and then stitch through all thicknesses, using a 1/8" seam. Leave the bottom open.

Stuff the BODY softly, stopping an inch from the bottom.

Lay the BODY faceup, sandwiching the tops of the LEGS between the body front and the back, as with ARMS. The baste line of the legs should be placed inside the stitch line of the body, and the leg seams should be positioned to the back of the body. Baste, then stitch the legs in place, using a 1/8" seam.

For finishing touches, glue white pom-poms on the face as eyeballs (the pattern shows the placement). For the iris, glue black 1/2" pom-poms in the centers of the white pom-poms.

Tie a bow, and glue it on as shown!

The Long-Legged Frog says:
Be proud of who you are. You're one-of-a-kind, so enjoy your unique self!

TWIG

(a variation of Long-Legged Frog)

Here the eyes have it: they're yo-yo's made of felt, and they're big and expressive. Wearing a heart instead of a bow tie, Twig is generally appealing to teenagers. His legs are made of faded blue jeans.

Materials
Body & feet: 9" X 12" of blue felt
Face: scrap of yellow felt
Hands: 8" X 8" piece of white felt
Arms: 9" X 9-1/2" piece of cotton print
  fabric
Legs: 10" X 13" piece of faded denim
Eyes: scraps of white, green, and black felt
Nose: black embroidery floss
Heart: scrap of red felt
Stuffing: polyester fiberfill and polystyrene
  beads

Pattern Pieces
(See pages 129–131.)
Cut:
BODY (2), FEET (4) from body color felt
FACE (1) from felt scrap
HANDS (4) from white felt
ARMS (2) from print fabric
LEGS (2) from faded denim
HEART (1) from red felt
EYES (6) from white, green, and black felt
  scraps (two circles of each color)

Directions

Cut out all pattern pieces.

Position the FACE on one BODY section. Keep the top edges even, and topstitch with red thread along the MOUTH LINE of the FACE. For the NOSE, make two French knots, as shown, using six strands of black embroidery floss.

Fold the ARM in half lengthwise with right sides together, and stitch, leaving both ends open. Turn the arm right side out. Repeat this step for the other ARM and the LEGS.

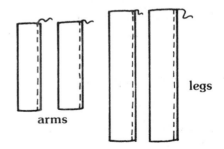

arms   legs

Pin the two HANDS together with the edges even. Sandwich the lower ARM between the two HANDS. Position the arm seam at the center back of the hand, and pin. Topstitch around the outer edge of the hand, taking a 1/8" seam. Repeat these steps for the other ARM and the LEGS.

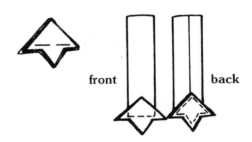

front   back

Stuff the ARMS and LEGS softly to within an inch of the top. Position the ARM and LEG seams to the center back. Baste raw edges together 1/2″ from the top.

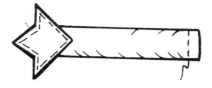

Place the BODY sections together with the edges even, and pin at the top. Sandwich the ARM between the BODY front and the back. (The ARM seam goes to the back of the body, and the baste line of the ARM will be inside the stitch line of the BODY.) Pin and stitch through all thicknesses, using a 1/8″ seam. Leave the bottom straight edge open.

Stuff the BODY softly, stopping an inch from the bottom. With the body faceup, sandwich the tops of the LEGS between the body front and the back (the baste line of the LEGS should be placed inside the stitch line of the BODY). The leg seams are positioned toward the back of the body. Baste, and then stitch the LEGS in place through all thicknesses, using a 1/8″ seam.

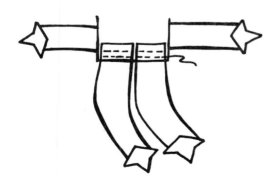

Fergus needs EYES. The next step is to make a yo-yo (stitch by hand).

Stitch around the edge of a white felt circle, put a wad of stuffing in the center, draw up the circle, and tie a knot. Repeat for the other eye, using the same amount of stuffing and drawing up the same. The yo-yo's should be the same size.

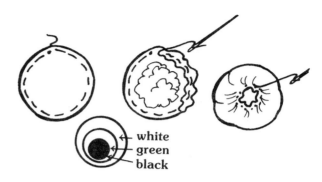

white
green
black

Position the eyes on the FACE, and blind-stitch them in place. Glue a green circle of felt in the center of each eye, and then glue the black circles as shown.
Glue the heart onto the left side of the body.

Twig says:
If you don't try, you've lost anyway.

59

FERGUS THE FROG

A little bit of appliqué adds a lot of princely charm to Fergus. Cotton prints and solids are suggested, but you might like the texture of satin, lightweight velvet, or a combination of the two.

Materials

Body back: 11″ X 15″ piece of print fabric
Body front: 11″ X 15″ piece of solid fabric
Heart: scrap of contrasting fabric
Face: two 1″ white pom-poms, and scrap of
    black felt or six strands of black embroidery
    floss.
Stuffing: polyester fiberfill

Pattern Pieces

(See pages 125-127.)
Cut:
BODY BACK (1), ARMS (2), FACE (1),
    from print fabric
BODY FRONT (1), ARMS (2), from
    solid-color fabric
HEART (1) from contrasting fabric

Directions

Cut out all pattern pieces.

To appliqué the FACE and the HEART on the BODY front, position the wrong side of the face to the right side of the body front, as shown. With the top edges even, pin in place. Position the wrong side of the heart to the right side of the body front, and pin securely. By hand or machine, appliqué the face and the heart to the body front, as

shown. For the NOSE, use six strands of black embroidery floss to make two French knots (or cut two small circles of black felt for the NOSE and then glue them on after the toy is stuffed).

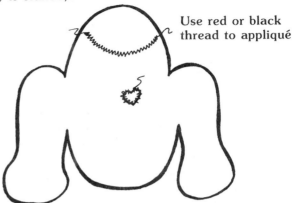

Use red or black thread to appliqué

With right sides together, pin one SOLID ARM to one PRINT ARM, keeping all edges even. Stitch as shown, leaving the top open to turn and stuff. Clip curves. Repeat for the other arm.

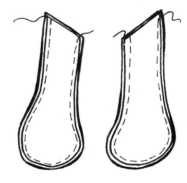

Turn the ARMS right side out, and stuff to within an inch of the top. Baste the top ARM closed, as shown. Position the ARMS on the BODY front, solid side of the arm to the solid side of the body front, and baste, as shown.

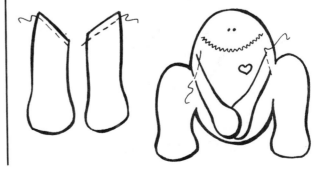

Pin the BODY, back to front, with all edges even. Being careful not to catch the lower ARMS in the stitching, stitch as shown, leaving a space open between the dots in order to turn and stuff. Clip curves, and turn right side out.

Stuff the LEGS first, then the FACE area. As you are stuffing, remember to use less stuffing near, and none in, the area diagramed as the stitch line. Turn in the raw edges of the opening, and whipstitch closed.

Before beginning the stitching that will give Fergus a more realistic shape, fold the ARMS up out of the way, with the FACE side up, and stitch through all thicknesses as shown. Backstitch at the beginning and the end to prevent raveling.

Now you're ready for the finishing touches. Glue pom-pom eyes in place. Cut circles of black felt, and glue them to the front of each pom-pom to make irises. If you want to glue on felt circles for the NOSE, this is the time to do so.

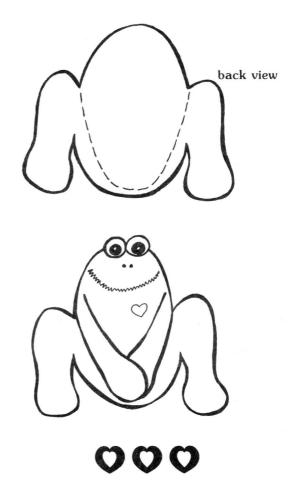

back view

Fergus the Frog says:
Isn't life just the perfect thing to pass the time?

SKINNY MINNIE

An old-timey rope doll, Minnie is "sew" easy to make out of scraps. She requires very little machine work. A small clump of flowers, purchased at a hobby shop, adds a nice finishing touch when placed in the knot that forms the hands.

Materials

Body: 5″ X 8″ piece of beige cotton
Dress: 6″ X 15″ piece of print fabric
Hat: 8″-diameter circle of print fabric
Shoes: 4-1/2″-diameter circles (2) of print fabric
Arms & legs: 36″ length of beige macramé cord
Hair: 9″ length of brown macramé cord
Eyes: black embroidery floss
Mouth & nose: pink embroidery floss
Neck band: 4″ length of decorative trim

Ribbon: enough to tie tiny bows on hair
Stuffing: small amount of polyester fiberfill

Pattern Pieces

(See pages 139-141.)
Cut:
BODY (2) from beige fabric
DRESS (1), HAT (1), SHOES (2) from assorted fabrics
NECK BAND (1) from decorative braid or trim
ARMS & LEGS from 36″ length of macramé cord

Directions

Cut out all pattern pieces.

Before removing the pattern from the cut pattern pieces, trace the FACE on the right side of one body section. (An alternative is to draw the face on freehand after the doll is done.)

Pin the BODY sections right sides together. Stitch, leaving the straight edge open as shown. Clip curves.

Turn right side out, and stuff firmly. Turn in the edge of the opening and slipstitch closed.

For HANDS, tie a knot in the center of the 36″ length of cord. Tie twice if you wish.

To form ARMS and LEGS, hold the knot ("hands") in the center, and make a loop about 9″ around. (Longer arms will mean shorter legs, so adjust to suit yourself.)

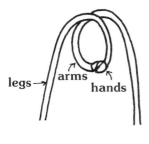 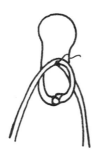

legs → arms hands

Tack the top of the loop securely to the center of the bottom of the body.

For FEET, tie a knot at each end of the cord, adjusting if necessary, to even up the legs.

If the bottom edge of the DRESS was not placed on the selvage, turn up and stitch a narrow hem on the wrong side of the DRESS. Optional: Stitch narrow lace along the hem of the DRESS.

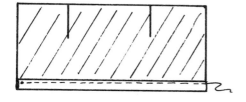

On the right side of the DRESS, pin 1/4″ ribbon or bias tape along the edges of the ARM slits (allow extra ribbon to turn at the bottom of the slit), and stitch a narrow seam. Clip to the stitching at the bottom of the slit. Turn the ribbon facing to the inside of the dress, then pin and stitch.

  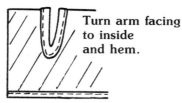

Stitch outside.

Turn arm facing to inside and hem.

Fold the DRESS in half with the right sides together, and stitch back seam as shown.

Turn the DRESS right side out. Slip the top of the DRESS up around the NECK of the doll, and place the ARMS in the arm slits. Run a basting stitch around the top of the DRESS, overlapping the front of the DRESS arm slit over the back arm slit by 1/4″ (see detail A in the illustration). Draw up snugly and knot. Adjust the gathers, making sure the ARM slits are lined up with the BODY side seams. Baste around the NECK again, attaching the DRESS to the BODY.

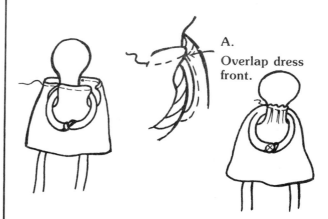

A. Overlap dress front.

With decorative braid, cover DRESS/NECK stitching. Pull snugly around the neck overlap in the back. Turn the end of the braid under, and tack it in place. Blindstitch around the neck again to attach the braid to the DRESS and to the BODY.

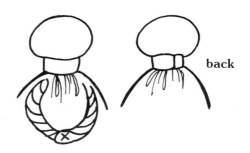

back

63

For the HAIR, tack the center of a 1″ length of cord or yarn to the top center seam of the head. Fold the ends down to make bangs. Separate the yarn strands for hair.

Tack the middle of an 8″ length of cord over the stitch holding the bangs. Tack HAIR along the front edge of the HEAD side seam as shown.

For a BONNET, run a gathering stitch as shown, and draw it up to fit the HEAD. Put a small amount of stuffing inside the stitched circle to give the hat a puffy shape. Pin the hat to the head, adjust the gathers, and stitch the hat to the head.

stuffing

Minnie's SHOES are yo-yo's.
To make a yo-yo, hold a fabric circle wrong side toward you, and turn under the fabric edge, as shown. Run a gathering stitch along the edge.

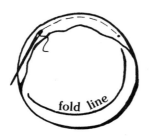

fold line

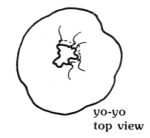

yo-yo
top view

Draw the yo-yo snugly up over the FOOT (the knot at the end of the leg), which will be encased inside the yo-yo. Adjust the gathers, and stitch the yo-yo to the LEG cord.

Pull to shape.

To shape the FOOT, squeeze the yo-yo lengthwise, as shown. (Check to see how the legs dangle; feet should face forward.) Take a stitch at the side, and take the thread over the top of the foot to the other side. Take a stitch, pull up as desired, and knot.

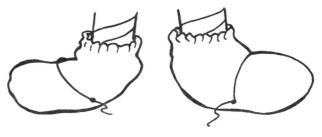

Now you can make the face. For the EYES, use two strands of black embroidery floss, and make two French knots. For the NOSE and MOUTH and CHEEKS, use one strand of pink embroidery floss. Work the nose and mouth in an outline stitch. The cheeks are in the lazy daisy stitch.
Tie tiny bows at the sides of the head where the stitching stops for hair attachment. Insert a small posy bouquet in the knot that serves as the hands.

BUNNY & CARROT

Easily made from fake fur and trimmed with pom-poms and scraps of felt, Bunny's just the right size to round out an Easter basket or to delight a little one at any time of the year.

Materials
Body: 12″ X 36″ piece of white fake fur
Ear lining: 6″ X 6″ piece of pink cotton
Face: two white 1″ pom-poms, one 1/4″ pink pom-pom, scraps of white and black felt
Tail: a 1″ white pom-pom
Bow: one foot of 1/2″- to 1″-wide ribbon
Carrot: scrap of orange felt, 24″ length of green yarn
Stuffing: polyester fiberfill

Pattern Pieces
(See pages 133 and 137.)
Cut:
BODY (2), EARS (2), POUCH (1) from BODY fabric
EAR LINING (2), POUCH (1) from lining fabric

EYES (2) from black felt
TEETH (1) from white felt
CARROT (2) from orange felt

Directions
Cut out all pattern pieces.

In making the BODY front, turn down the top edge of the wrong side of the POUCH, and stitch a 1/4″ hem.

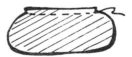

Pin the EAR LINING to the EAR, right sides together. Stitch, leaving the bottom open. Clip curves, and turn right side out. Repeat for the other ear.

Fold the EAR edges in slightly, as shown, and baste the raw edges closed.

Pin the EARS, lining side to the right side of one BODY section, centering the EARS at the notches, as shown. Baste the raw edges together.

Pin the wrong side of the POUCH to the right side of the BODY section (same section as EARS are on) with the side and bottom edges even. Baste as shown (see previous illustration).

Pin the BODY front to the remaining BODY section, right sides together. Stitch as shown, leaving the bottom open between the dots. Clip curves.

Turn the BODY right side out. Stuff the ARMS and LEGS, softly, almost to the stitch lines. Stitch by hand or machine through all thicknesses, just as shown.

Stuff the BODY, turn in the edges of the opening, and then stitch closed.

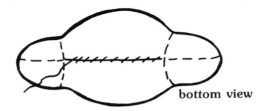

bottom view

Glue the TEETH in place on the face.

Glue pom-pom CHEEKS at the top of the teeth.

Center the NOSE at the top of the cheeks.

Position the EYES on the FACE, above the cheeks, and attach.

Place the pom-pom TAIL as shown, and glue it in place. Tie the BOW around the neck.

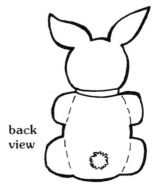

back view

To make the CARROT, fold a 24" length of green yarn in random lengths, as illustrated below, and tack the ends together.

Pin the two layers of the CARROT together, with the raw edges even, and insert the tacked ends of the yarn LEAVES between the top of the CARROT layers. Pin and stitch, leaving an opening between the dots.

Stuff softly, and close the seam.

Put the carrot in the bunny's pouch.

Bunny says:
Though the love you feel for a stuffed toy isn't returned, still it is real love.

COTTON BUNNY

A variation of Bunny & Carrot, Cotton Bunny is for younger children. This washable version replaces the pom-poms and felt details with embroidery and yo-yo's. (See the first chapter in the book for help with embroidery stitches and yo-yo construction.)

Materials
Body, ears, pouch, tail: 12″ X 36″ piece of cotton print (Soft colors and tiny prints work best.)
Ear lining: 6″ X 6″ piece of pink fabric
Face: Black, pink, and white embroidery floss
Bow: a foot of ribbon 1/2″- to 1″-wide
Carrot: scrap of orange fabric and 24″ length of green yarn for leaves
Stuffing: polyester fiberfill

Pattern Pieces
(See pages 133 and 137.)
CUT:
BODY (2), EARS (2), POUCH (2), TAIL (1) from BODY fabric
EAR LINING (2) from lining fabric
CARROT (2) from orange fabric scrap

Directions

Cut out all the pattern pieces.

To make the POUCH, place right sides together with edges even. Stitch as shown, leaving the bottom edge open. Clip the top corners, and turn right side out. Press.

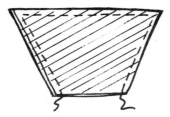

On the right side of the BODY section with the FACE, pin the corners of the top edge of the POUCH at the dots (where the LEG meets the BODY SIDE). Keep the bottom edge of the pouch even with the body, and edge-stitch the pouch to the body as shown.

Pin the body front to the body back with right sides together and all edges even. Stitch as shown, leaving the bottom open between the dots. Clip curves.

Turn the BODY right side out, and stuff the ARMS and LEGS almost to tack lines. Stuff the BODY smoothly, but use less stuffing where tacking will be done.

Turn in the bottom edges (1/4″) and blind-stitch them closed. Use crochet thread or yarn to make tie tacks as shown.

bottom view

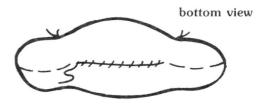

Embroider the face as illustrated or as you wish.

Satin stitch 2 strands of embroidery floss for eyes—black, nose—pink, and teeth—white

Backstitch/outline-stitch 1 strand black embroidery floss for whiskers and mouth lines

To make the TAIL, stitch a baste line 1/4″ from the outer edge of a yo-yo. Put a wad of stuffing about the size of a walnut in the center of the yo-yo (on wrong side of fabric), and draw up (the tighter the circle is drawn up, the smaller the tail will be). Knot. Position the tail low at the center back, and blindstitch in place. If this bunny is for a small child, stitch around several times, knotting occasionally to prevent raveling.

To make the EARS, pin the EAR LINING to the ears, right sides together. Stitch as shown, leaving the bottom straight edges open. Trim the tips of the ears almost to the stitching, and clip curves.

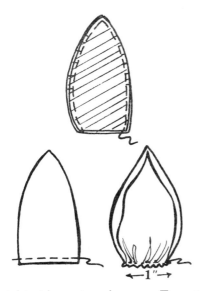

Turn right side out and press. Turn in 1/4" and baste the bottom edges of the EARS together. Draw up the stitching to about 1" and knot. Evenly position the EARS on the HEAD, and stitch securely in place.

To make the CARROT, pin the carrot layers, right sides together. Stitch, using a 1/8"

seam as shown. Leave open between the dots. Clip curves.

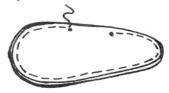

Turn the CARROT right side out, and stuff softly. Turn in the raw edges, and blindstitch the opening closed.

For the LEAVES, make random-length loops, the longest being about 6". Loop some thread around the center as shown. Hand-stitch the center of the loops securely to the top of the CARROT. Fold the leaves up together, and loop the thread around the base of the leaves a few times, knotting securely. Place the carrot in the pouch.

Tie the BOW around Cotton's neck, and it's playtime.

69

MR. HUGS & MRS. KISSES

Do our clowns look complicated? Do you like a challenge? Well, these clowns are not really complicated, but they can be as challenging as you wish to make them. Each is about 30 inches tall, but believe it or not, each is made from one white cotton work sock—the kind with a narrow band of elastic at the top. Stuffed tubes of fabric for arms and legs give the illusion of hugeness. The outfits can be pieced together, like a quilt top, with each piece a different color, or you could use patchwork-printed fabric for everything but the ruffle. You might like to add appliqué to sleeves or front. Creating the face can be as simple as gluing black felt circles for eyes, a red circle nose and mouth, or a felt appliqué and embroidery.

Throughout this book, we have given many examples of facial features and expressions. This clown couple will give you a chance to try your wings—a do-your-own-thing project.

If you've never worked with socks in toy building, I can tell you it's fun. Each creation will be one of a kind because no two socks will be exactly the same size, partly because the amounts of stuffing used will vary. Be sure to make the stuffing firm and smooth.

If you're new to toymaking, practice on one of the easier patterns in this book before tackling Mr. Hugs and Mrs. Kisses.

The hair looks difficult to do, but it's nothing more than rectangles of pinked fabric pinched in the center and randomly stitched to the head.

Suit diagram: 4 print rectangles, each 12″ X 30″

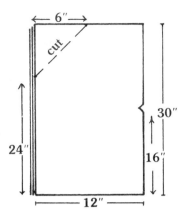

Sleeves:
2 squares, each 18″ X 18″

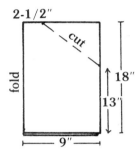

Ruffle: one length of fabric 10″ X 45″ (fabric width selvage to selvage)

MR. HUGS

Materials

Body: white cotton work sock, men's size
Arms & legs: 1/2 yard of 36″-wide red-and-white-striped fabric
Hands: 6″ X 20″ piece of white fabric
Feet: 6″ X 32″ piece of black or navy fabric
Hair: 1/3 yard of red cotton fabric cut with pinking shears into 2″ X 5″ rectangles
Hat: a scrap of bright cotton print
Face: red, pink, black, and white felt scraps; a red 1″ pom-pom; black and white embroidery floss
Stuffing: polyester fiberfill
Suit: 1-1/2 yards of a cheery print or a bright solid-color fabric
Ruffle: 10″ X 45″ piece of contrasting fabric, hook and eye or 29″ length of ribbon for neck closure
3/8″-wide elastic for neck

Pattern Pieces

(See page 143.)
Cut:
ARMS (2), LEGS (2) from red-and-white-striped fabric
HANDS (2) from white fabric
FEET (2) from black or navy fabric
HAIR from 1/3 yard of 36″-wide red cotton cut with pinking shears into 2″ X 5″ rectangles
HAT (1) from bright cotton print
SUIT (4) from rectangles of print fabric, each 12″ X 30″
SLEEVES (2) from 18″ X 18″ squares
RUFFLE (1) from contrasting fabric

Directions

Cut out all pattern pieces.
HEAD AND BODY: Turn the sock wrong

side out, fold the heel as shown, and stitch across.

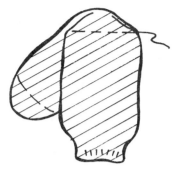

Turn the sock right side out (sock will now be straight, with no heel). Stuff to within an inch of the top. By hand, run a basting stitch 1/2" down from around the top of the sock. Push the top 1/2" of sock to the inside as you draw up the stitching tightly. Knot securely.

top of sock

Since socks vary in size, you will have to decide where the placement of the face should be. There's a diagram below to help you. The stitched heel will be to the back of the head.

The bottom of the MOUTH should be at least 2-1/2" above the heel line, which serves as the NECK line.

Place the NOSE about 5-1/2" down from the sock top. Move felt facial features around until you are pleased with their placement. Pin in place. Secure the felt features by embroidery, blindstitching, or glue. Detail with additional embroidery if you wish.

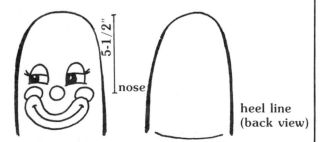

5-1/2"

nose

heel line (back view)

To make the HAT, fold right sides together, and stitch along the straight edge as shown.

fold

Turn the hat right side out, and stuff. Run a basting stitch 1/4" from the raw edge, and draw up the stitching just so edges tuck under easily. Position on the head as you see fit (we placed the hat toward the back of the head), and pin or hold the hat in place to baste the hat to the head. Stitch around again to secure.

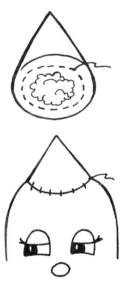

Now you can attach the HAIR. Start around the base of the hat, one hair rectangle at a time. Pinch the center, wrap the thread around, and stitch to the head at 1/2" to 1" intervals, working down on the head. The

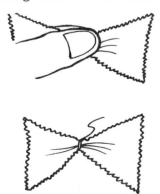

bottom row of hair will be at about the center of the cheek line.

LIMBS: Assemble the ARMS and LEGS as follows. Pin the straight edge of the HAND to the short straight edge of the arm, with right sides together (stripes go around the arms and legs). Turn the seam toward the hand, and topstitch as shown.

Fold the arm with right sides together, stitch as shown, and clip curves. Repeat these steps for the other arm and the legs.

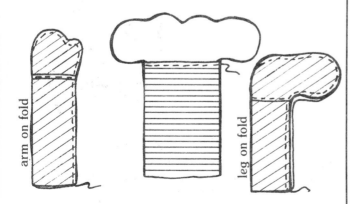

Turn right side out. Stuff the hands and FEET firmly, but use less stuffing in the arms and legs. To keep the limbs soft and floppy, soft-stuff to within an inch of the tops of the arms

and legs. Turn in the raw edges and baste together.

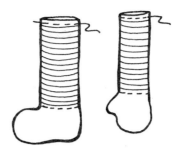

Pin the LEGS to the side of the BODY as shown, and stitch them securely to the body. Pin the arms to the side of the body about an inch below the neck. Make sure the arms are evenly placed, and stitch them securely to the body.

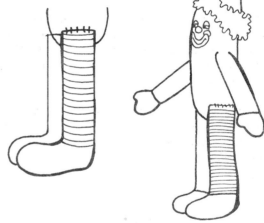

CLOTHING: On the wrong side of the SLEEVE, turn up a 1/4" hem (see **a** below). About 1-3/4" from the bottom edge of the sleeve, pin the bias tape (see **b** below). Stitch close to the edges of the bias tape, leaving the ends open. Through this casing, thread 1/4" elastic to fit the arm measurement plus 1". Baste the ends of the elastic in place (see **c** below).

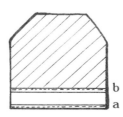 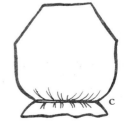

73

Pin the two main sections of the SUIT FRONT with right sides together (decide which will be the front), and stitch from the NECK edge to the notch at the CROTCH, as shown (curving into crotch).

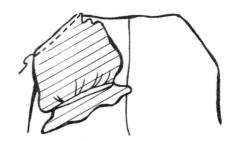

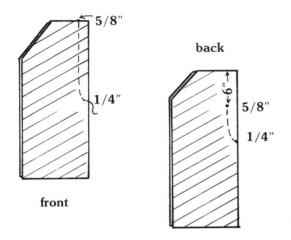

back

front

5/8"

1/4"

6"

5/8"

1/4"

With right sides together, pin the remaining slanted edge of the sleeve to the slanted edge of the back, and stitch.

Pin the two sections of the SUIT BACK with right sides together. Measure 6" down from the neck. Baste. Use a 5/8" seam to stitch on down, curving to a 1/4" seam at the crotch, as shown.

Press the back seam open from the neck to the center seam, and turn under 1/4" on each side of the hem for facing. See the illustration below.

To make the UNDERARM and SIDE SEAMS, place right sides together, fold sleeve, and pin the edges even, front to back. Stitch the underarm and side seams as shown. Repeat for the other side.

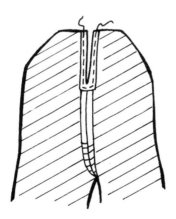

Hem and gather the bottom of the LEG, turn up a 1/4" hem on the wrong side of the leg, and stitch. Pin bias tape 2" from the hem. Stitch close along both edges of the tape, leaving the ends open for a casing. Thread 1/4" elastic through the casing to fit the leg measurement plus 1". Baste the ends of the elastic in place.

With right sides together, pin the slanted edge of the SLEEVE to the slanted edge of the front, and stitch. Repeat for the other side.

For the INNER LEG seam, fold the front to back with right sides together, pinning the inner leg edges even. Stitch as shown. Clip almost to the stitching line at the crotch.

On the RUFFLE, turn under a 1/4″ hem to the wrong side. By machine, run a basting stitch along the center of the ruffle.

See instructions for simplified attachment of RUFFLE on page 79.

Turn the suit right side out, and then turn down the NECK edge 1/4″ on the outside, and baste.

Draw up the basting stitch of the ruffle to match the size of the neck edge. Do not fold the ruffle. On the wrong side of the neck edge, pin the neck to the baste line of the ruffle with the right sides together, keeping the ends of the ruffle and the back edges of the suit even. Stitch along the neck edge, allowing a 1/8″ seam.

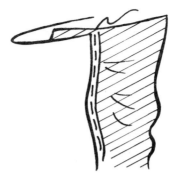

To form a CASING, turn the suit right side out. At back neck edge, open the ruffle. Approximately 1-1/2″ down from the neck/ruffle stitching, pin the ruffle to the suit, and stitch around. Note: The ruffle may be gathered, but the suit should lie smooth. Leave both ends open so you can thread the 3/8″ elastic through the casing. Adjust to fit the neck of the clown. Stitch the ends of the elastic in place.

 casing

Finish the suit by sewing a hook and eye to the top back neck edge. An alternative for the neck closure is to attach ribbon ties at the neck opening.

♥ ♥ ♥

Mr. Hugs says:
Put a little love in your heart.

MRS. KISSES

Materials

Body: white cotton work sock, men's size

Arms & legs: 1/2 yard of 36"-wide red-and-white-striped fabric

Hands: 6" X 20" piece of white fabric

Feet: 6" X 32" piece of black or navy fabric

Hair: 1/2 yard of red cotton fabric cut with pinking shears into 2" X 6" rectangles

Face: pink, white, and black felt scraps; a red 1" pom-pom; red and black embroidery floss

Stuffing: polyester fiberfill

Dress: 1 yard of a cheery print fabric

Neck ruffle: 10" X 45" piece of contrasting fabric

Apron: 13" X 16" piece of contrasting fabric

1/4"- to 3/8"-wide elastic for sleeves, neck, bloomer legs, and waist

Hook and eye or 24" length of ribbon for neck closure

Bloomers: 14" X 44" piece of bloomer fabric

Trim as you wish with lace, rickrack, or a rufffle around the hem of the dress. Some big silk flowers will add a special touch.

*If you plan to add a ruffle at the hem, shorten the dress length by the width of the ruffle.

*Dress: 16" X 45" piece of fabric; fold selvage to selvage; fold again, with the folded edge turned to the selvage. Cut the armhole from the folded side.

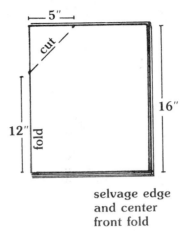

**selvage edge
and center
front fold**

Apron: 13" X 16" piece of fabric folded and cut along selvage edge to form curve

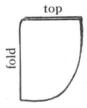

Sleeves: 2 squares, each 16" X 16", folded and cut along selvage edge

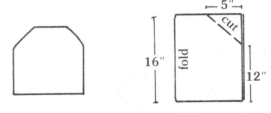

Bloomers: 14" X 44" length of fabric folded with selvage edges together

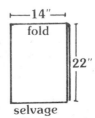

Ruffle (at neckline): one length of fabric 10" X 45" (fabric width selvage to selvage)

Pattern Pieces

(See pages 143-147.)
Cut:
ARMS (2), LEGS (2) from red-and-white-striped fabric
HANDS (2) from white fabric
FEET (2) from black or navy fabric
HAIR from 1/2 yard of 36"-wide red cotton cut with pinking shears into 2" X 6" rectangles
DRESS (1) from 16" X 45" print fabric
SLEEVES (2) from rectangles of print fabric, each 16" X 16"
NECK RUFFLE (1) from contrasting fabric
APRON (1) from lightweight fabric
BLOOMERS (2) from white or contrasting fabric

Directions

Cut out all pattern pieces.

Turn sock wrong side out and fold heel, as shown. Stitch across heel.

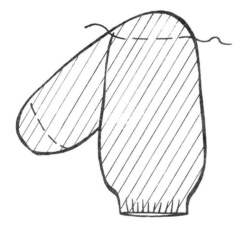

Turn sock right side out (sock will be straight with no heel). Stuff firmly and smoothly to within 1" of the top. By hand, baste around the top of the sock. Draw up stitching tightly, and push the top edge of the sock inside. As you draw up stitching, knot securely.

top view

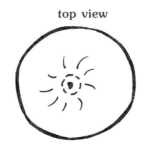

HEAD AND BODY: Since socks vary in size, you will have to decide where the placement of the face should be. There's a diagram below to help you. Stitched heel should be at the back of the head. The bottom of the MOUTH should be at least 1-1/2" above the heel line, which serves as the NECK line. Place the NOSE about 5" down from the sock top. Move felt facial features around until you are pleased with the placement. Pin them in place. Secure felt features by embroidery, blindstitching, or glue; add more embroidery if you wish.

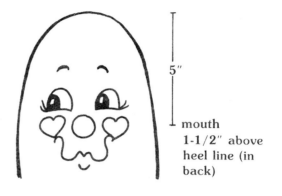

5"

mouth
1-1/2" above
heel line (in
back)

To attach the HAIR, start around the top center of the HEAD. One hair rectangle at a time, pinch the center, wrap the thread

around, and stitch to the head at 1/2" to 1" intervals, working down the head. The bottom row of hair will be at about the center of the cheek line.

back view

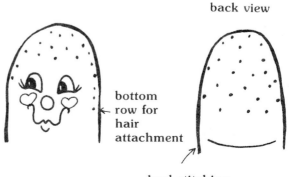

bottom
row for
hair
attachment

heel stitching

LIMBS: Assemble the ARMS and LEGS as follows. Pin the straight edge of the HAND to the short straight edge of the arm, with right sides together. (Stripes go around arms and legs.) Turn the seam toward the hand, and topstitch as shown.

Fold the arm with right sides together, stitch as shown, and clip curves. Repeat these steps for the other arm and the legs.

Turn right side out, and stuff hands and FEET firmly. Stuff the arms and legs less firmly so that they will be floppy. Soft-stuff to within 1" of the top of arms and legs. Turn in raw edges and baste together.

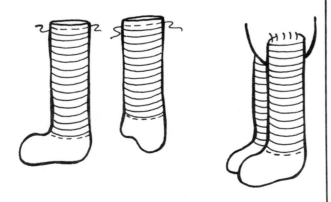

Pin legs to the side of the body, as shown, and stitch securely to the body. Pin arms to the side of the body about 1/2" below the

"neck." Make sure arms are evenly placed; stitch securely to the body.

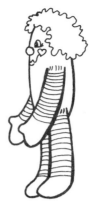

CLOTHING: With the right side of the APRON to the right side of the lace, gather and baste the lace along the curved edge of the apron; stitch in place. With apron right side up, press the lace right side out. Topstitch along the edge of the apron as shown.

To gather the upper edge of the apron, machine-baste 1/4" from the edge as shown.

Adjust gathers to fit the top edge of the dress front. Start and end the apron 1/4" from armhole seam line as shown; baste the apron to the dress front.

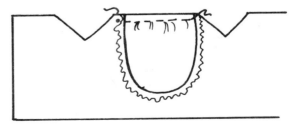

Finish the lower edge of the SLEEVE with a narrow hem, or if you wish, add lace. On the wrong side of the sleeve, measure and mark 1-1/2" from the hem for the elastic guide (casing). Pin bias tape along that line and stitch close along both edges of the tape. Leave the ends open. Thread elastic through the casing and adjust to measure 1" more than the clown's wrist measurement. Stitch both ends of elastic in place. (Experienced seamstresses can omit the casing by stretching and stitching elastic in place.)

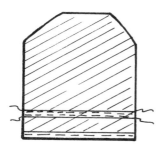

Fold the sleeve with the right sides together; pin and stitch the underarm seam as shown. Turn right side out.

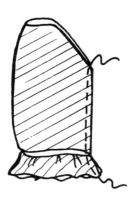

With right sides together and edges even, pin the slanted edge of the sleeve to the slanted edge of the dress armhole. (The underarm seam of the sleeve should meet the bottom of the "V" in the dress armhole, and the top straight edge of the sleeve should be even with the neck.) Stitch the sleeve to the dress, backstitching at the beginning and end of stitching (at neck edge). Clip "V" (underarm seam) almost to the stitching.

Go to the next step for the ruffle.

Narrowly hem both long edges of the NECK RUFFLE, adding rickrack, if desired. Machine-baste along the center of the ruffle, gather to fit the dress neck, and pin the wrong side of the neck edge along the basting line of the ruffle. With the ends of the ruffle and the dress back edges even (ruffle will have some gathers), stitch the DRESS to the ruffle.

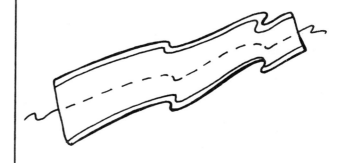

To form a CASING, leave the dress faceup, and fold the ruffle over to the right side of the dress (neck seam, just stitched, forms the top of the casing). The casing should be about 1/2" wide. Using the previous stitching as a guide, pin the ruffle down on the dress, and stitch through the ruffle and the dress (the ruffle will be gathered a bit, but the dress should lie smooth). Thread 3/8" elastic through the casing, adjust to fit the clown's neck, and stitch the ends of the elastic in place. Sew a hook and eye for a neck closure. An alternative is to attach ribbon ties at the neck opening.

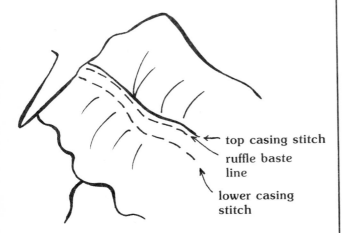

top casing stitch

ruffle baste line

lower casing stitch

Finish the bottom of the dress with a 1″ hem, or add trim if you wish.
Fold the dress with right sides together, and pin the back edges even. Stitch as shown.

Now it's time to construct the BLOOMERS. With right sides together and the edges even, stitch one curved edge as shown (this will be called the center front seam). Clip curves.

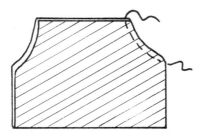

To make the WAISTLINE casing, press under a 1″ hem to the wrong side of the upper

edge, then pin and stitch. Thread elastic through the casing. Adjust to fit the clown body, plus 1″. Tack the ends of the elastic.

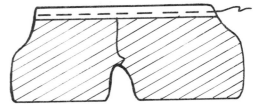

To finish the LEG edges, make a narrow hem or add trim. On the wrong side of the bloomers and 2″ up from the leg hem, mark a line as an elastic guide. Pin bias tape along the guide line, and stitch close along both edges. Leave the ends open to thread elastic through. Adjust to fit plus 1″. Tack the ends of the elastic.

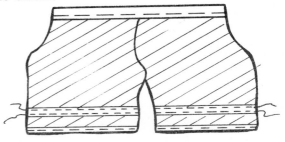

To make the back center seam, fold the bloomers with right sides together and back edges even, and then pin and stitch as shown. Clip curves.

For the INNER LEG seam, fold the bloomers right sides together, center back to center front seam. Pin the leg edges evenly and stitch as shown.

Soft Toys Album

Twins Bonny and Bobby love to be cuddled
by their Mama and Papa Bo-Bear. When
Sugar Pops and Honey Pot have chores, the
babies rest together in their blankets.

This delicate pillow case is soft and sweet - just right for the sleeping head of mother's tiny treasure.

This basket of fruit is sure to heal any ailing heart. The bright inedibles bring smiles and good cheer to any home they visit.

Always prepared in case Mr. McGregor is in the garden, Bunny tucks his carrot into his pouch for every trip – whether to the back yard for the afternoon or to Grandma's for an overnight.

Mr. Hugs and Mrs. Kisses get rave reviews for every performance. No other clown couple has ever warmed so many hearts.

Eyes popping and polka-dots dancing, Fergus the Frog and his alter ego poise for their next leap - right into your heart. These fellows deserve warm hugs. Ready. Set. Ribbet!

Sock and glove complement each other in these smiling friends. Terry-textured Bell-Ve-Deer gives a smug grin and shows off his Christmas ties to his visitor, Glovey, Dear.

Terri Mouse assumes multiple personalities as he scavenges for cheese and clues to the whereabouts of stealthy cats.

This dandy trio of sports, attired in their spring finery of checks and dots, offers a smile and a hearty "Hello" to passersby.

Sunning on lilypads of imaginary pools are our long-legged frog friends who hang and dangle by their webbed feet and hands.

Customized cars mean you'll "travel" in style with automobiles you design yourself. Stripped or loaded with fancy features, they'll transport you to creative adventures.

Skinny Minnie and her slender sisters string along in the simplest way. "There's not much to us," they proclaim, but they've won many a heart for proving "sew" simple.

Felt and fantasy collab-
orate as creatures from
sea and space rendezvous
for smooth sailing.

Clamity Jane will cache
a collection of secrets,
jewelry, hair barrettes,
and other small valuables.

Pillow Pals

Although these designs were first conceived as basic pillows and nothing more, my children opened my eyes to the infinite possibilities for these designs. I simply drew the pattern for daughter Deanna and said, "Here are some scraps of felt; see what you can do with them. Your brother can help decorate." She cut, sewed, and stuffed the car design, and then they were ready for the fun part—decorating. Andy chose button hub caps and easy glue-on felt or stickers for decoration. Deanna loves to embroider. She asked me to draw a design for her, and then she added her choice of colors, stitch patterns, and extra detail to come up with a truly delightful creation. They were so excited that they decided to make a whole fleet of cars, each one different. If small pillow shapes can be decorated, think how much easier it would be to decorate larger shapes; and how about large wall hangings or a mural of cars going around the room? (See pages 91-93 for helpful grids.) The simple idea was just a seed, and turned over to children to plant, it grew into delightfully unique creations. Yea for kids!

PLAYFUL PILLOW IDEAS FOR ALL AGES AND STAGES

Rather than give a single pattern in one size, I've included grids or graphs to enable you to make each pillow in a variety of sizes.

For an infant, make the pillow shape small enough for tiny fingers to grasp, but not small enough for the baby to choke on. The tiny basic shape makes ideal first toys. Remember the safety rules and the importance of washable fabrics, for tiny folks will put everything into their mouths. Felt is not suitable for infant toys. Use a more durable, washable fabric like cotton.

For pillows used as room decor, felt is bright, colorful, and easy to work with. Refer to pages 16 and 17 for general instructions on how to work with felt.

Flatsy construction applies to all of these pillow designs. This means two pieces of fabric will be cut exactly the same size and shape. One piece will be the front of the pillow; on the right side of this piece, work detail—by whatever method you choose—to give definition to the pillow. The other piece of fabric will be the back side of the pillow; leave it plain or decorate it as you like.

Definition may be added in a variety of ways: Work detail on the front of the pillow before sewing the front to the back.

Leave an opening, preferably along a straight edge, big enough to turn the pillow right side out easily.

After applying decoration to the pillow front, turn the right side of the pillow front to the right side of the pillow back, all edges even. Stitch, using a 1/4″ seam, leave an opening along a straight edge, and clip curves. Turn and stuff, then whipstitch the opening closed. Some decorations are easier to apply after the pillow is stuffed: On teen pillows, add glitter, buttons and bows, and fun stickers. Let your imagination run free.

Use embroidery for infant toys. Simply trace the detail on the right side of one pillow section (the front). Embroider the lines to give cartoon simplicity to the pillow shape, then proceed to assembly work.

If you use fabric paint, use nontoxic, waterproof, colorfast paints. Some kinds come in a tube; others are applied with a brush. Use what you feel comfortable with. Paint the detail on the right side of the front pillow section. When the paint is dry, proceed to assemble the pillow.

Appliqué is a colorful method to add definition to pillows and may be done by hand or machine, prior to pillow assembly.

Look for ways to use decorative laces and trims for added texture, but remember rules of safety.

For infant pillows, make some small pillow shapes and then some larger ones, soft and huggable.

Make baby shapes small, cut from felt scraps, stitch and stuff softly, and string for mobile, out of baby's reach.

Personalize baby pillows with the statistics—name, birth date, and weight. Simply write large enough to embroider easily over the lines.

Bottle: Trace lines, embroider with outline stitch, work letters in satin stitch. For an element of surprise, embroider the word EMPTY on the pillow back.

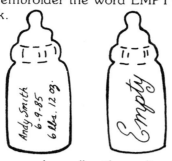

Pacifier: This design works well with appliqué. Cut two pieces of yellow calico; the right side of one section will be the pillow front. On pillow front, appliqué contrasting prints over the sections indicated. Ready for assembly.

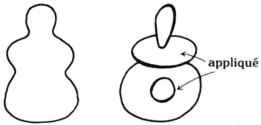

Gingerbread Boy: This pillow is cute in light brown calico. Embroider the face and add a heart or two. After the pillow is stuffed, tie a big bright bow around his neck.
Use embroidery or washable fabric paint detail.

B-A-B-Y Pillow: Cut two shapes; the right side of one will be the pillow front. Trace the letters and appliqué them to the right side of the pillow front. The "floral" centers of the letters could be purchased appliqués stitched securely in place.
This is cute as a wall hanging or as a room decor pillow of felt, lace, and trim. It is not a child's toy.

Bunny: Use a soft cotton print fabric for infants. Simply outline-stitch embroidery detail on the right side of one section (pillow front). If the pillow is for older children, stitch silk flowers and a bow at the base of the ear, after the pillow is stuffed.
Cut pillow shapes from acrylic fur and use a narrow zigzag machine stitch in a contrasting color to define lines on the pillow front. Add a pom-pom nose and bow for older children.

When making youth pillow designs, remember that all are flatsy shapes; the front and back are the same. Decoration can be plain or fancy. It's up to you. Look for unusual fabric texture, and don't be afraid to mix textures. Use any method of decoration you choose: appliqué, embroidery, paint. Mix felt and fur to vary texture in appliquéd work.

Animals: If the pillow isn't too large, add a pom-pom for the nose for added interest and dimension. Stitch an old metal dog tag securely to the dog's collar; appliqué acrylic fur ears and spots on the dog pillow front.

Candy Cane: From calico prints of red and white to acrylic fur, this can be a fun Christmas decoration, and don't forget to tie a big green bow around the pillow after stuffing.

All flatsy shapes of teen pillows are given dimension by the addition of appliqué, embroidery, or paint to the pillow front.

Make fun shapes from fun fabrics. Try fake fur, vinyl, and felt. Mix textures for interest.

Add rhinestones or glitter to the dial of the telephone or to the star.

Write and embroider a message on these pillow shapes.

Make them BIG for a big statement or small as "sun catchers" or mobiles. Add a chain for a key ring. These are great projects for teens to learn to sew and decorate. Use felt for these small projects.

Car: Boys may enjoy "customizing" the car shape. Make an "AUTO-mobile" with small car pillows made from scraps of felt, stuffed softly, and decorated with stickers, felt, or glitter.
Do I have to tell teens how to decorate a car? I think not—be innovative.

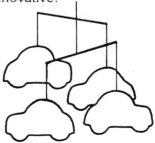

Kiss: Use satin or a cotton print with hearts. Write a message, embroider, or paint.

 # 1: Appliqué # to the right side of the pillow front. Personalize with a name or message. Use felt fabric.

Rainbow: This is easily made from appliquéd felt. Cut two pillow shapes of yellow felt. Cut one inside curve of blue felt. Cut one outside curve of red felt; stitch in place on the front of the pillow. Place the pillow front on the pillow back, stitch a narrow seam around the edge, and leave an opening as shown. Stuff softly; close seam. After stuffing, stitch little rainbow-colored bows randomly across the pillow.

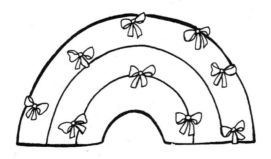

Man in the Moon: Simply embroider the outline, stitch facial features on the pillow front, and proceed to assemble.

Telephone: That'll be the day when a grandmother has to tell a teenager how to decorate a telephone!

Cut the pillow shapes from felt or any other fabric easily appliquéd. Cut a receiver shape and dial from a fabric of different texture, decorate the dial with hearts, rhinestones, or buttons, or write a message, then paint or embroider.

The little dissatisfaction which every craftsman feels at the completion of a design forms the germ of a new work.

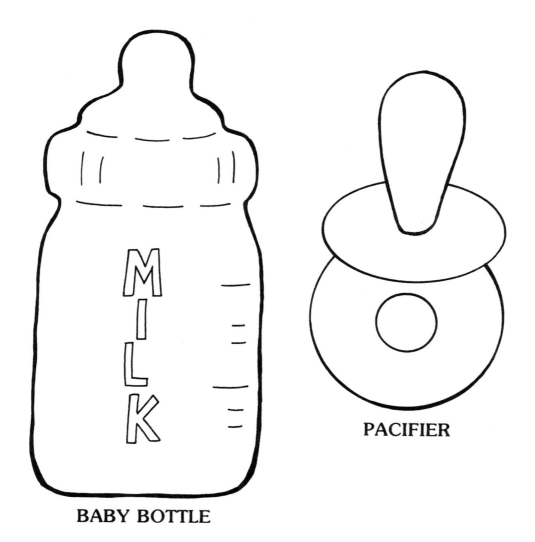

BABY BOTTLE

PACIFIER

B-A-B-Y PILLOW

BUNNY

GINGERBREAD BOY

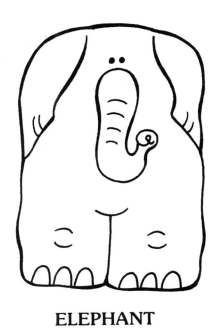

ELEPHANT

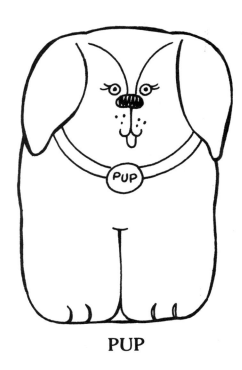

PUP

LION

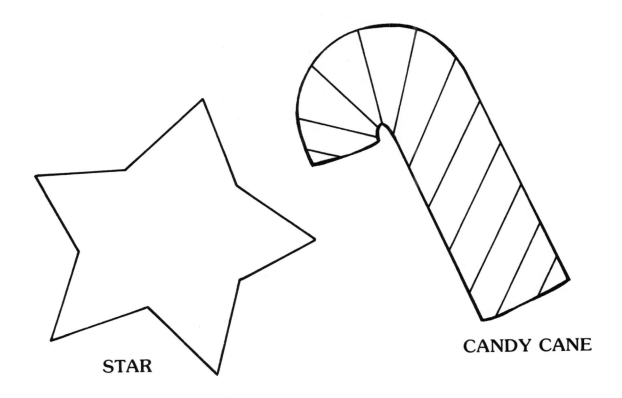

STAR

CANDY CANE

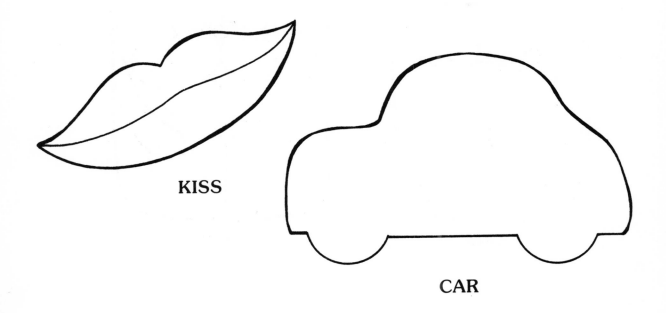

KISS

CAR

1

MAN IN THE MOON

RAINBOW

TELEPHONE

Embroidered Baby Pillow

The delicate airy appearance of this pillow top was achieved by using one strand of embroidery floss for all embroidery work. The oversized lazy daisy (see embroidery stitches on page 14) flower petals lend extra softness and detail.

① The pillow is constructed of two rectangles of soft cotton fabric 9″ X 10-1/2″. Pin the right sides together, with all edges even. Stitch as shown, leaving an opening at one end to turn. Clip corners, turn, stuff smooth and soft, and then close the opening by machine or whipstitch by hand.

The pillow case is constructed from one piece of soft semi-sheer cotton/blend fabric 10″ X 30″. Use 1/4″ seams on both pillow and case.

② Fold the pillow case in half, right side out, trace the design onto the front, and position "Baby" 2 inches from the fold centered top to bottom. Work the letters in a satin stitch. The flower petals are oversized lazy daisy stitches. Centers of flowers are French knots. Outline-stitch leaf lines in light green. Remember to use single strands of floss for all embroidery work.

After completing embroidery work, ③ turn right sides together, as shown, stitch long edges with 1/4″ seam, then backstitch at each end. Finish the hem as you choose, edge with lace, ribbon, and added embroidery work as illustrated in my granddaughter's pillow, or turn under 1/4″, then turn under again (1-1/2″) to hem.

1/2″

3/4″

1″

NOTES:

Patterns

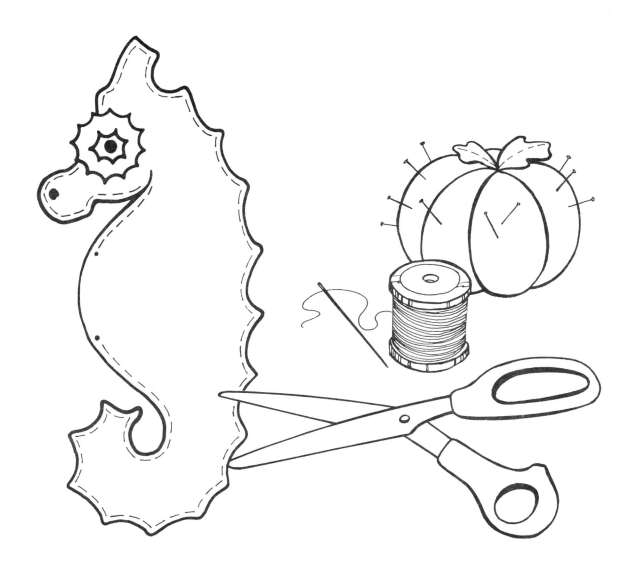

THE PATTERNS

This section contains the pattern pieces for all the toys except the pillows, which are grouped on pages 81–94.

For full-size pattern pieces, simply place tracing paper directly over the pattern. Then, holding the paper in place, carefully trace the lines, using a sharp No. 2 pencil. Don't forget to mark any darts, notches, or lines that will guide you in constructing a toy. Label each pattern piece, and note the number of each piece to be cut, as well as the direction of the arrows if the material has nap, design, or an uneven weave.

PATTERN MARKINGS AND TERMS

Cutting line: Cut along this line.

Fold line: Place the pattern along the folded edge of fabric.

Grain line: Place the pattern piece along the straight grain of the fabric. (Note: Felt has no grain, so it can be cut in any direction.)

Nap: Fabrics with one-way designs (such as paisley or flower prints), pile (a downy-textured surface, as in fur and velveteen), nap (in which the fabric's surface has been brushed to create a soft, fuzzy texture, as in flannel), or shading (as in satin fabric) must be cut so that the pattern pieces are laid in the same lengthwise direction, usually with the smooth side of the nap running down.

Notches and circles: Use these symbols for matching the pattern pieces. Cut outward at the notches; cutting inward could weaken the seam.

Seam allowance: This is the distance between the cutting and seam lines. (This book uses a 1/4″ or 1/8″ seam allowance.)

Seam line: Stitch along this line. All pattern pieces have the seam lines built in, so there's no need to add to the outside edge.

Shading: Shaded areas indicate that the wrong side of the fabric is out; white areas indicate the right side of the fabric.

CUTTING AND MARKING

Place the fabric with the right sides together, selvage to selvage, to make sure the fabric lies smooth. Arrange your pattern pieces so as to have the least amount of wasted fabric. Arrows on pattern pieces show the grain line for the correct directional placement on the fabric.

You may prefer to trace around small pattern pieces, rather than pinning the pattern to the fabric. I use table knives to hold large pattern pieces in place during cutting.

If you don't feel particularly confident or creative, you might choose to trace facial features lightly onto the fabric after the face is cut out, but before you begin construction. After the toy is stuffed, however, you'll get a better idea of where to place the face. (For help in making faces, turn to pages 13 and 28.)

METRICS

Measurements are stated in inches and feet. If you are familiar with the metric system, here is the conversion chart.

LINEAR MEASURE

1 inch = 2.54 centimeters
12 inches (1 foot) = 30.48 centimeters
3 feet (1 yard) = 91.4 centimeters

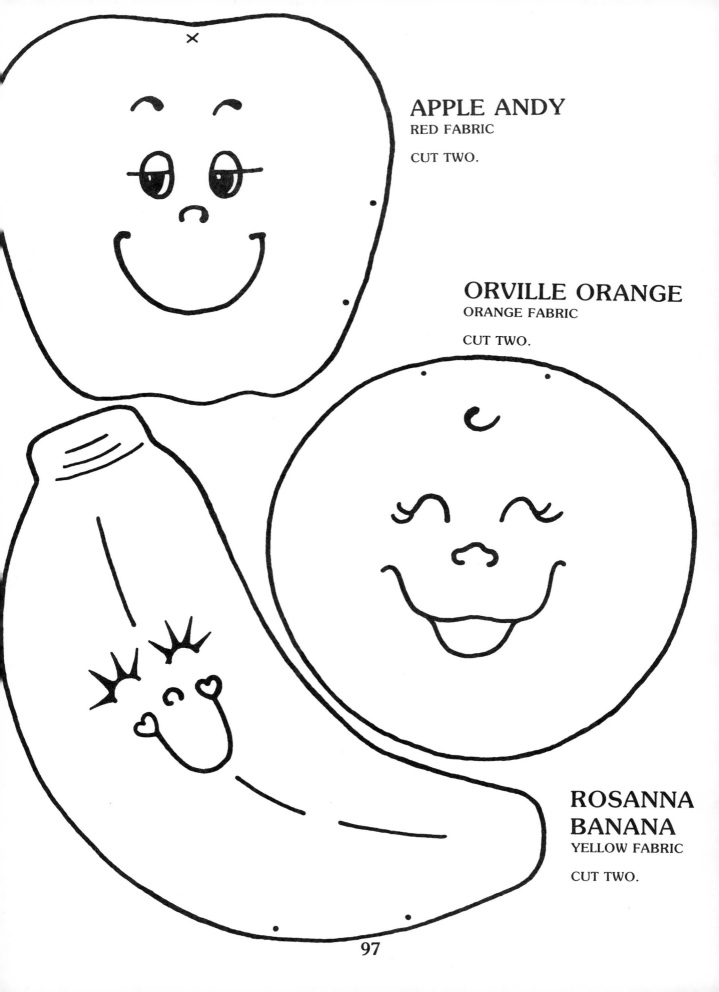

APPLE ANDY
RED FABRIC

CUT TWO.

ORVILLE ORANGE
ORANGE FABRIC

CUT TWO.

ROSANNA BANANA
YELLOW FABRIC

CUT TWO.

97

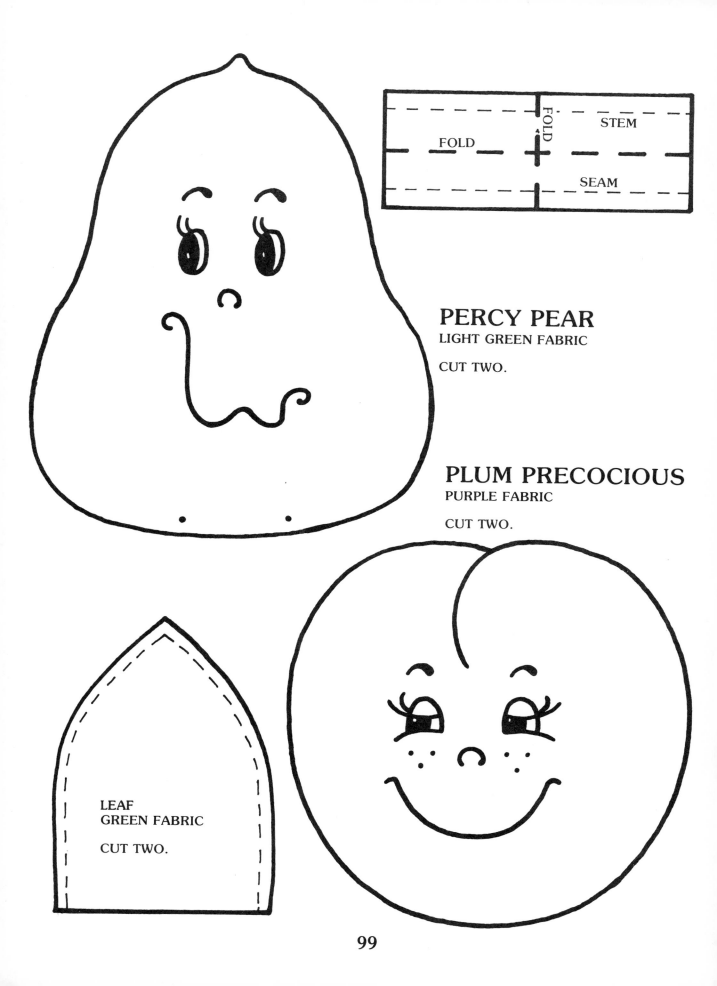

PERCY PEAR
LIGHT GREEN FABRIC

CUT TWO.

PLUM PRECOCIOUS
PURPLE FABRIC

CUT TWO.

FOLD

STEM

FOLD

SEAM

LEAF
GREEN FABRIC

CUT TWO.

99

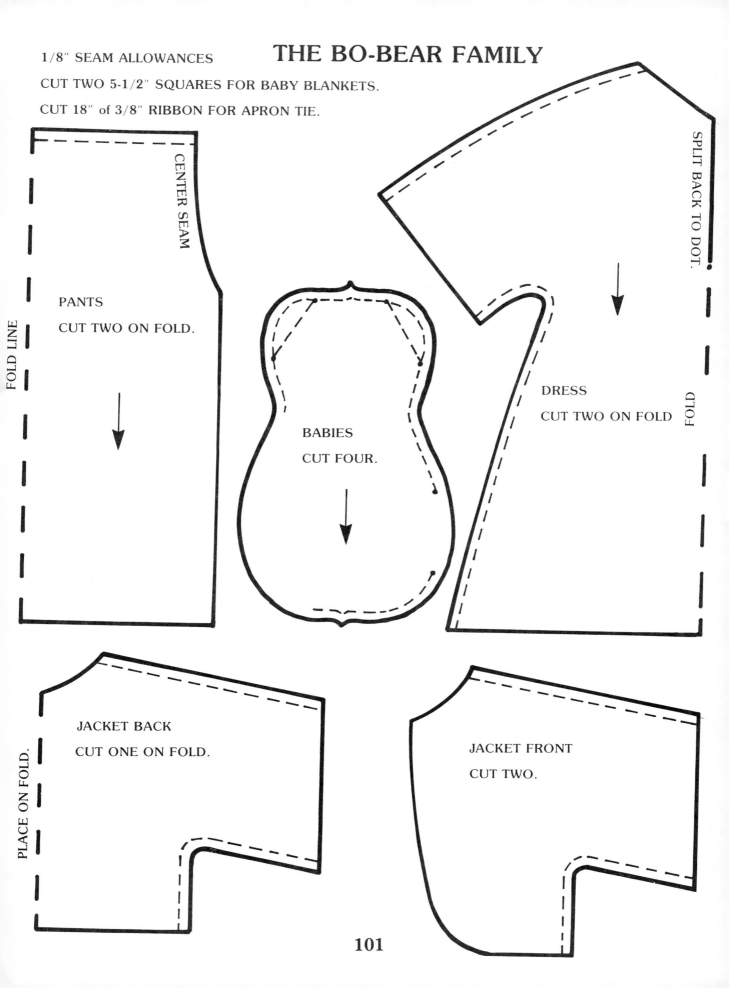

THE BO-BEAR FAMILY

1/8" SEAM ALLOWANCES

CUT TWO 5-1/2" SQUARES FOR BABY BLANKETS.

CUT 18" of 3/8" RIBBON FOR APRON TIE.

SPLIT BACK TO DOT.

CENTER SEAM

FOLD LINE

PANTS

CUT TWO ON FOLD.

BABIES

CUT FOUR.

DRESS

CUT TWO ON FOLD

FOLD

JACKET BACK

CUT ONE ON FOLD.

PLACE ON FOLD.

JACKET FRONT

CUT TWO.

101

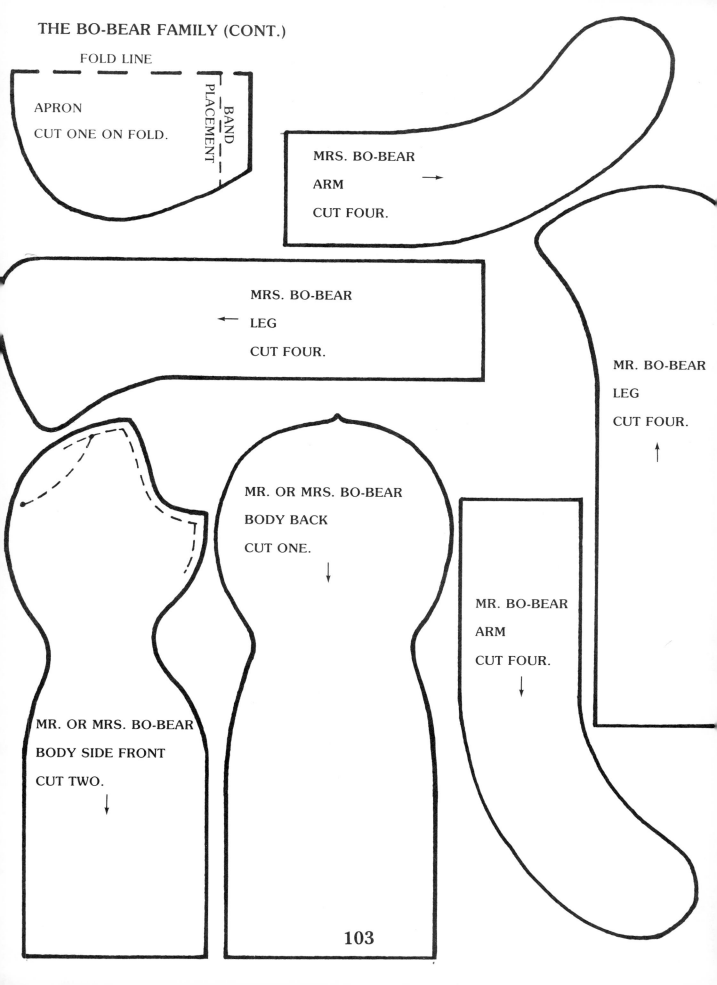

THE BO-BEAR FAMILY (CONT.)

FOLD LINE

APRON

CUT ONE ON FOLD.

BAND PLACEMENT

MRS. BO-BEAR

ARM

CUT FOUR.

MRS. BO-BEAR

LEG

CUT FOUR.

MR. BO-BEAR

LEG

CUT FOUR.

MR. OR MRS. BO-BEAR

BODY BACK

CUT ONE.

MR. BO-BEAR

ARM

CUT FOUR.

MR. OR MRS. BO-BEAR

BODY SIDE FRONT

CUT TWO.

103

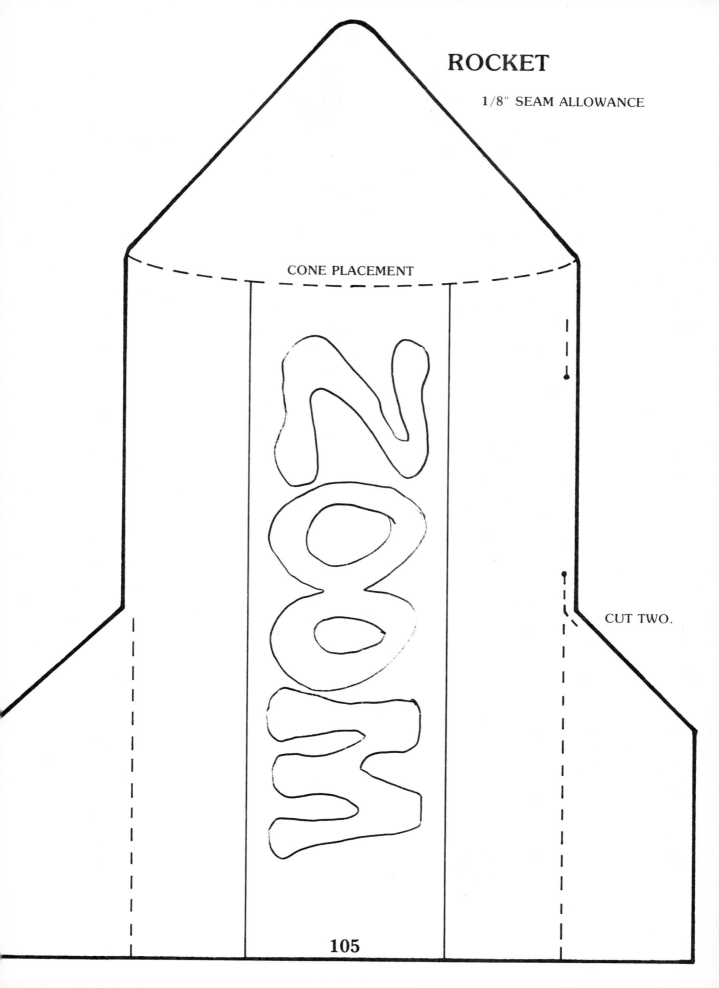

ROCKET

1/8″ SEAM ALLOWANCE

CONE PLACEMENT

CUT TWO.

105

ROCKET (CONT.)

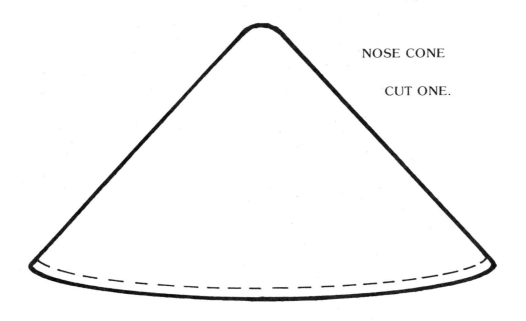

NOSE CONE

CUT ONE.

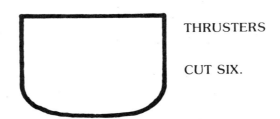

THRUSTERS

CUT SIX.

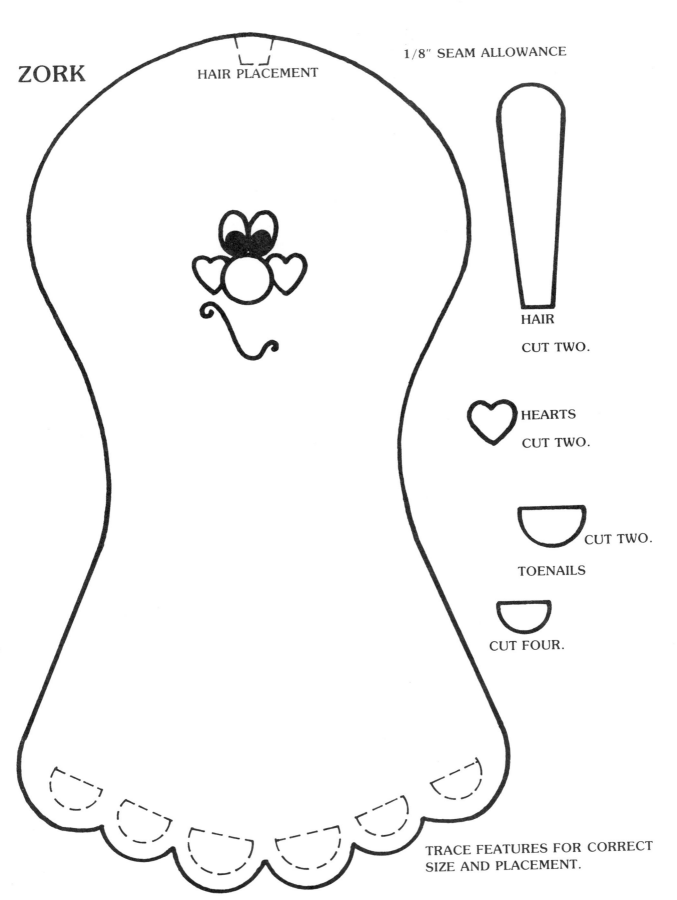

ZORK

HAIR PLACEMENT

1/8" SEAM ALLOWANCE

HAIR
CUT TWO.

HEARTS
CUT TWO.

CUT TWO.

TOENAILS

CUT FOUR.

TRACE FEATURES FOR CORRECT
SIZE AND PLACEMENT.

MEECH

1/8" SEAM ALLOWANCE

HAIR PLACEMENT

HAIR

CUT ONE.

ON FOLD

CUT

TOENAILS

CUT TWO.

CUT TWO.

111

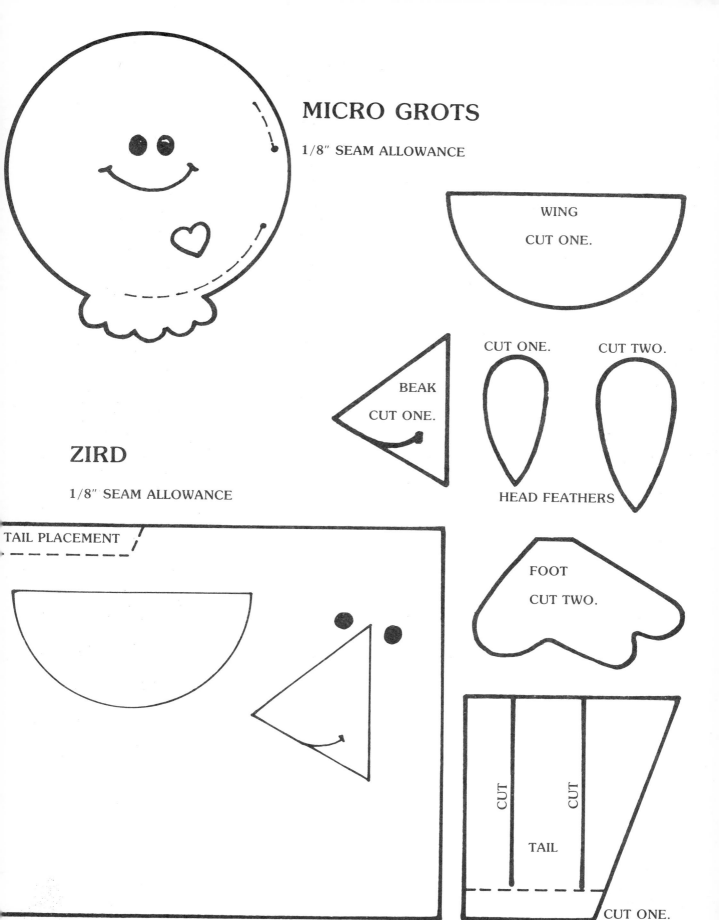

MICRO GROTS

1/8" SEAM ALLOWANCE

WING

CUT ONE.

CUT ONE.   CUT TWO.

BEAK

CUT ONE.

ZIRD

1/8" SEAM ALLOWANCE

HEAD FEATHERS

TAIL PLACEMENT

FOOT

CUT TWO.

CUT

CUT

TAIL

CUT ONE.

113

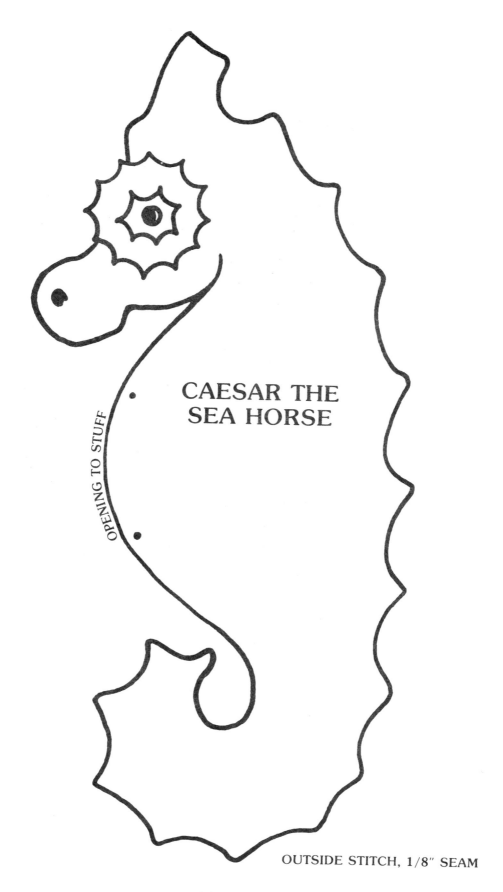

CAESAR THE
SEA HORSE

OPENING TO STUFF

OUTSIDE STITCH, 1/8″ SEAM

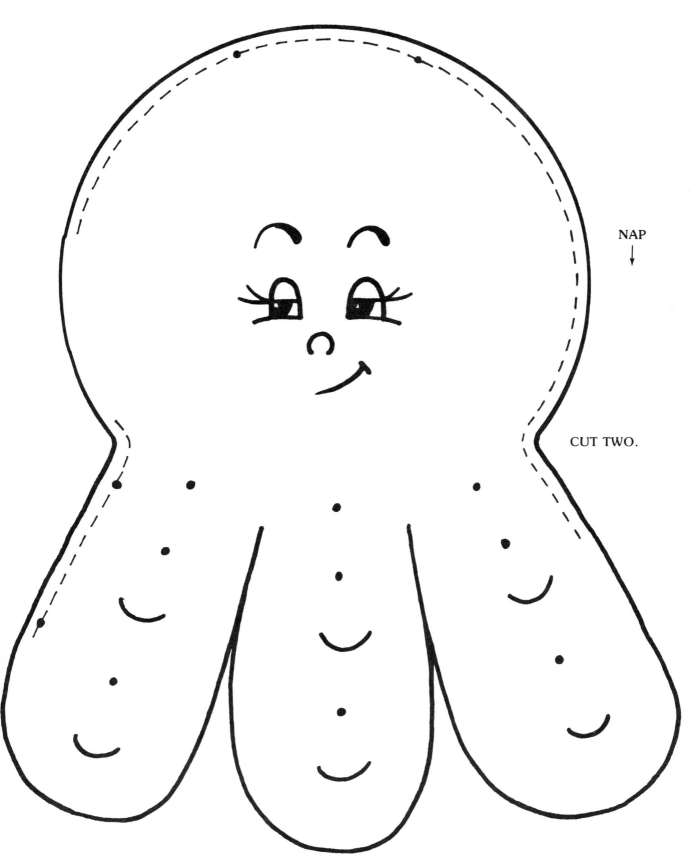

NAP

CUT TWO.

OGGIE OR AGGIE OCTOPI

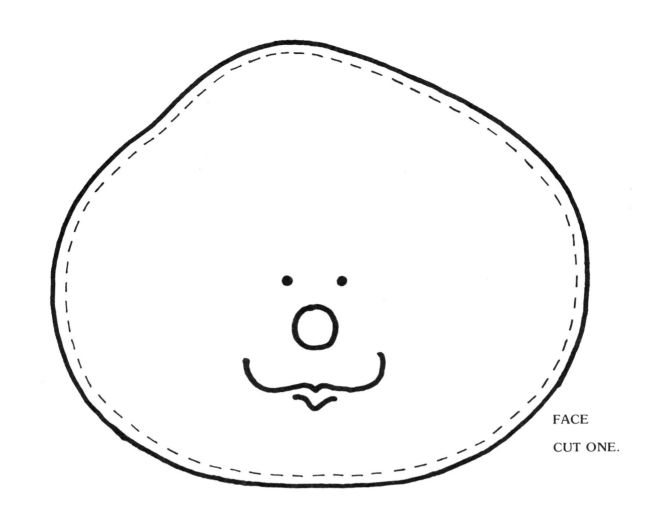

FACE

CUT ONE.

CLAMITY JANE

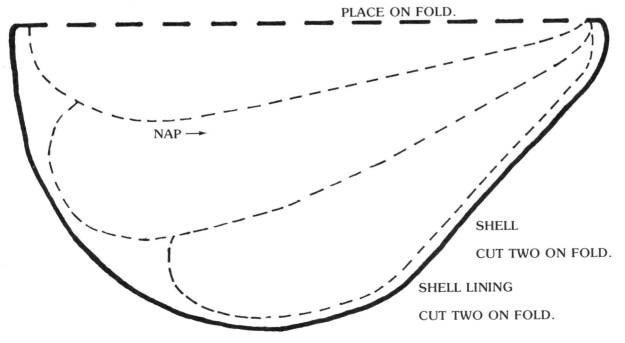

PLACE ON FOLD.

NAP →

SHELL

CUT TWO ON FOLD.

SHELL LINING

CUT TWO ON FOLD.

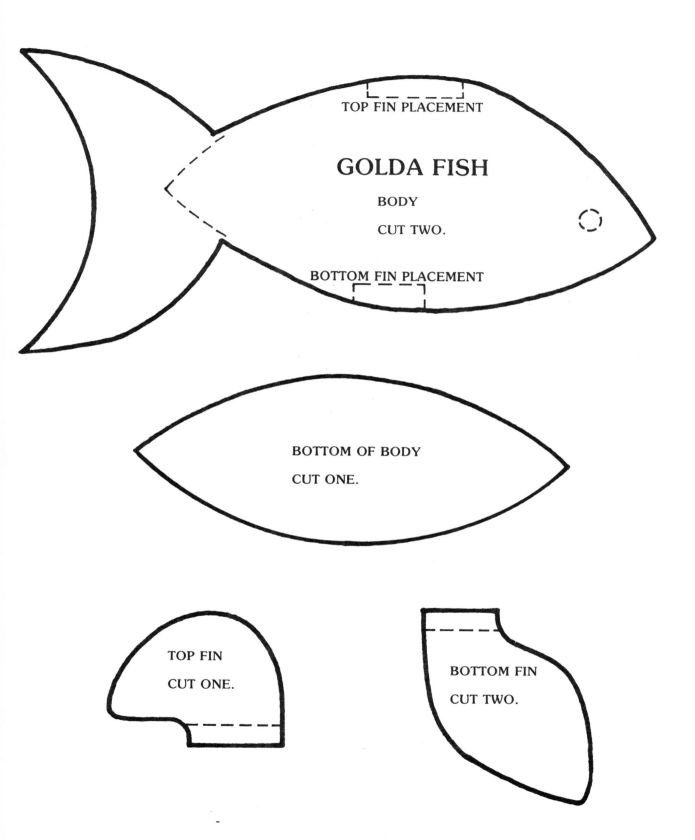

TOP FIN PLACEMENT

GOLDA FISH

BODY

CUT TWO.

BOTTOM FIN PLACEMENT

BOTTOM OF BODY

CUT ONE.

TOP FIN

CUT ONE.

BOTTOM FIN

CUT TWO.

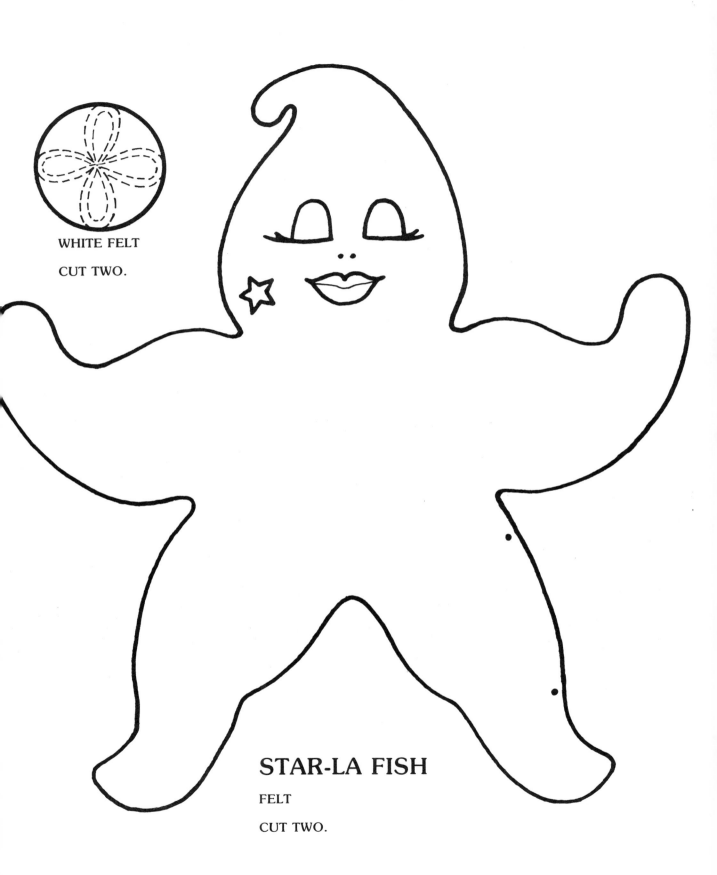

WHITE FELT

CUT TWO.

STAR-LA FISH

FELT

CUT TWO.

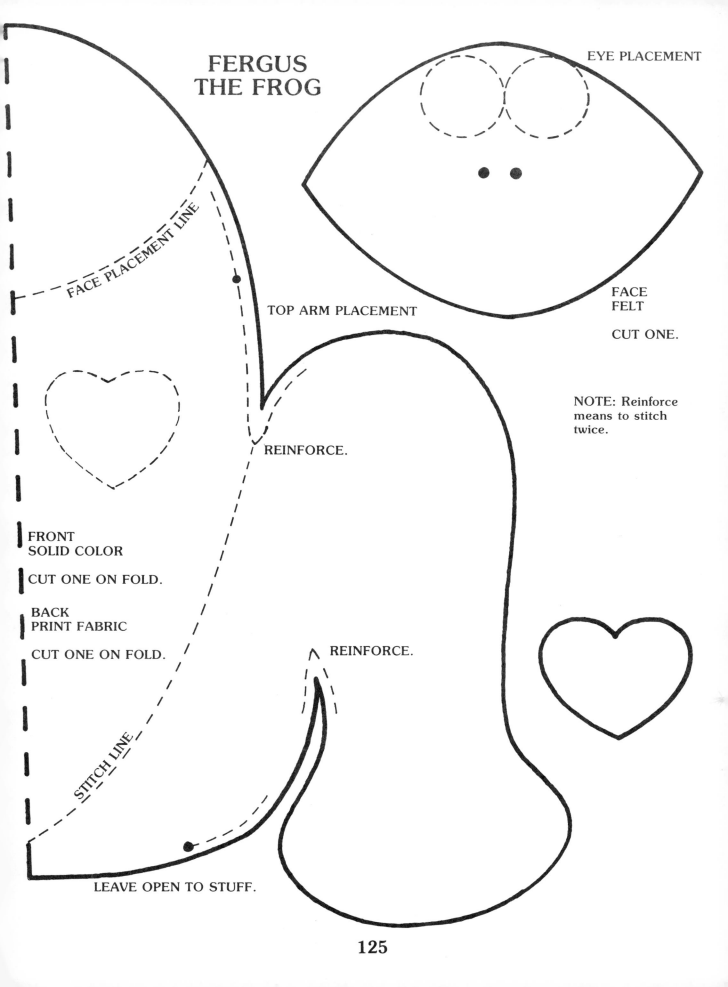

FERGUS
THE FROG

EYE PLACEMENT

FACE PLACEMENT LINE

TOP ARM PLACEMENT

FACE
FELT

CUT ONE.

NOTE: Reinforce
means to stitch
twice.

REINFORCE.

FRONT
SOLID COLOR

CUT ONE ON FOLD.

BACK
PRINT FABRIC

CUT ONE ON FOLD.

REINFORCE.

STITCH LINE

LEAVE OPEN TO STUFF.

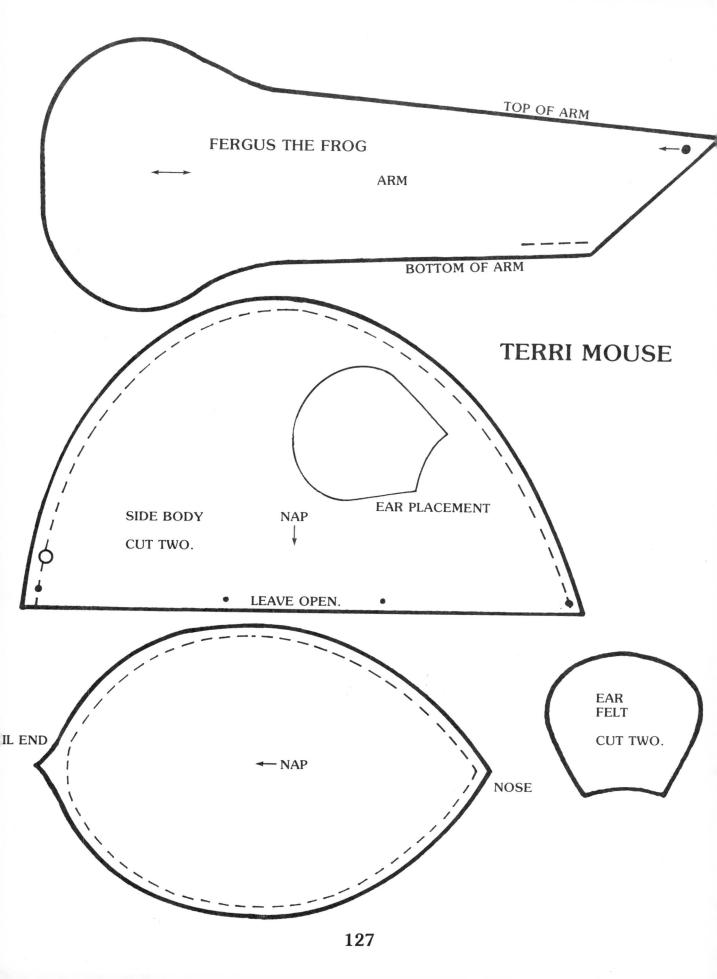

FERGUS THE FROG

ARM

TOP OF ARM

BOTTOM OF ARM

TERRI MOUSE

SIDE BODY

CUT TWO.

NAP

EAR PLACEMENT

LEAVE OPEN.

IL END

NAP

NOSE

EAR
FELT

CUT TWO.

127

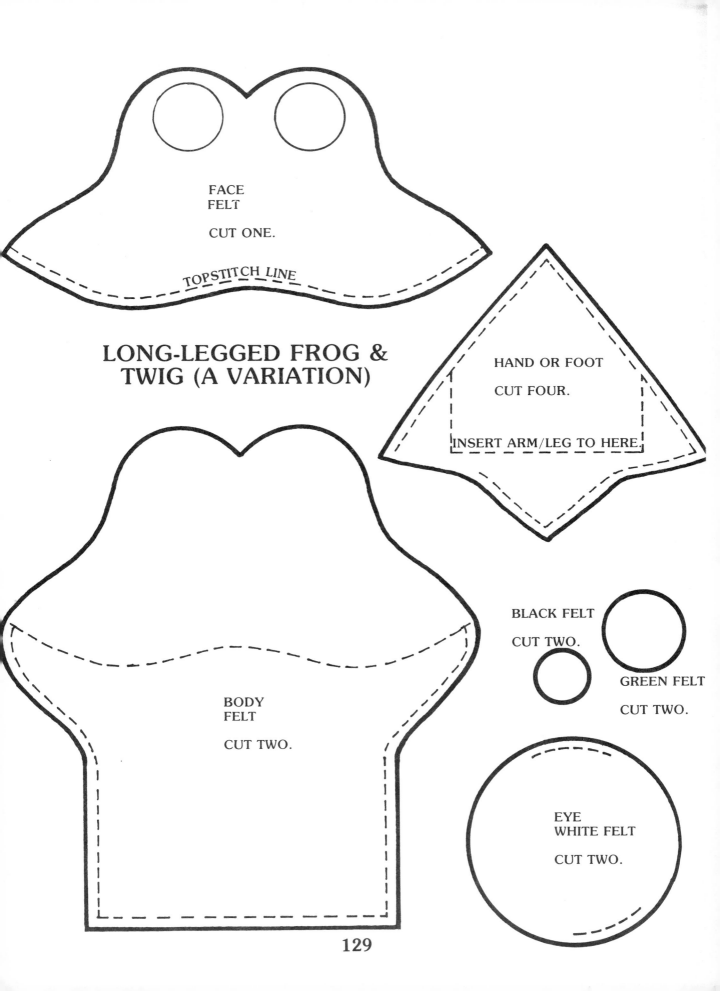

FACE
FELT

CUT ONE.

TOPSTITCH LINE

LONG-LEGGED FROG &
TWIG (A VARIATION)

HAND OR FOOT

CUT FOUR.

INSERT ARM/LEG TO HERE.

BLACK FELT

CUT TWO.

GREEN FELT

CUT TWO.

BODY
FELT

CUT TWO.

EYE
WHITE FELT

CUT TWO.

129

SEAM ALLOWANCE

SEAM ALLOWANCE

LONG-LEGGED FROG AND
TWIG (A VARIATION)

SEAM ALLOWANCE

SEAM ALLOWANCE

LEG
PRINT FABRIC

CUT TWO.

ARM
PRINT FABRIC

CUT TWO.

CENTER FOLD

CENTER FOLD

CENTER EAR CENTER EAR

BUNNY & CARROT
BODY

CUT TWO.

NAP
↓

133

NOTE: Accessory
pattern pieces
appear on page
137.)

PUPPY LUV

CUT TWO.

135

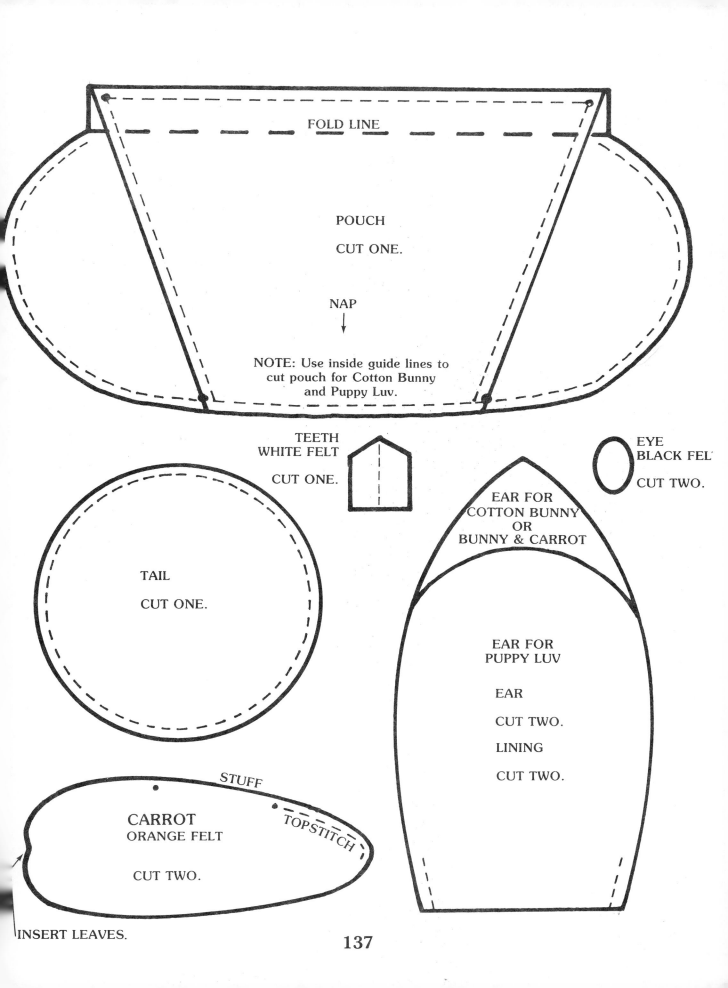

FOLD LINE

POUCH

CUT ONE.

NAP

NOTE: Use inside guide lines to
cut pouch for Cotton Bunny
and Puppy Luv.

TEETH
WHITE FELT

CUT ONE.

EYE
BLACK FELT

CUT TWO.

TAIL

CUT ONE.

EAR FOR
COTTON BUNNY
OR
BUNNY & CARROT

EAR FOR
PUPPY LUV

EAR

CUT TWO.

LINING

CUT TWO.

STUFF

CARROT
ORANGE FELT

TOPSTITCH

CUT TWO.

INSERT LEAVES.

137

SKINNY MINNIE

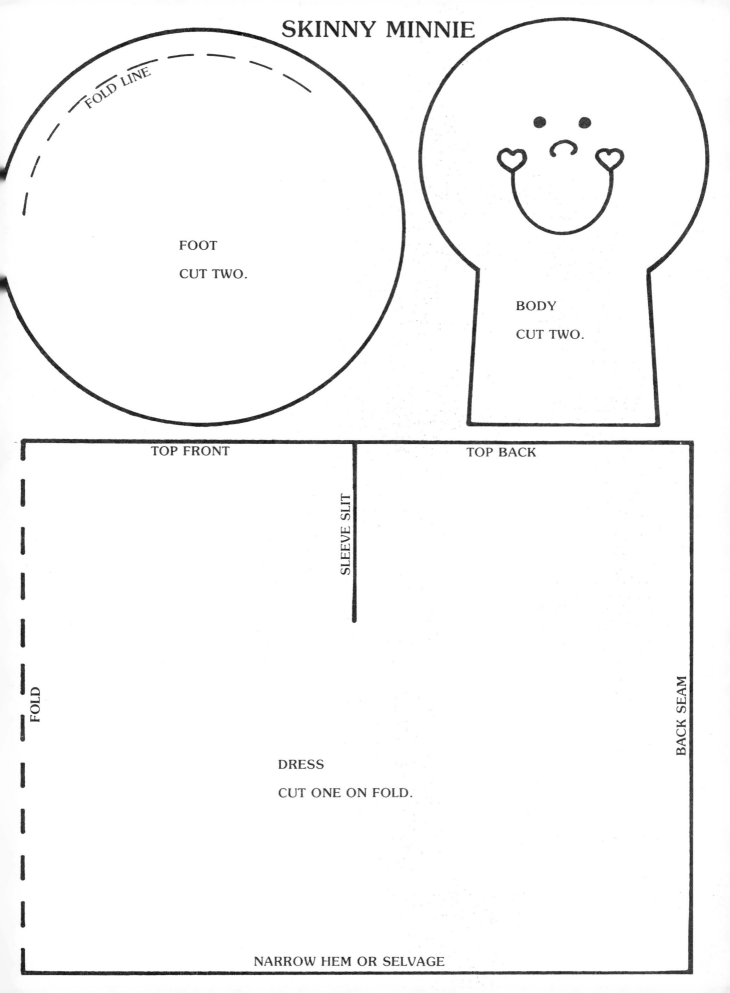

FOLD LINE

FOOT

CUT TWO.

BODY

CUT TWO.

TOP FRONT

TOP BACK

SLEEVE SLIT

FOLD

BACK SEAM

DRESS

CUT ONE ON FOLD.

NARROW HEM OR SELVAGE

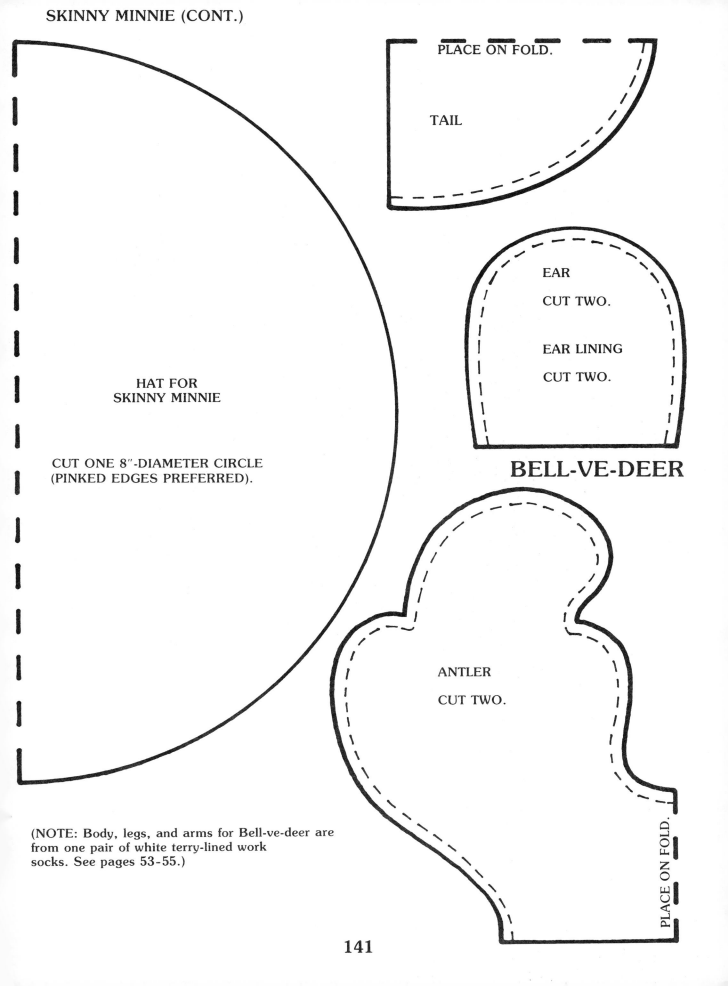

PLACE ON FOLD.

TAIL

EAR

CUT TWO.

EAR LINING

CUT TWO.

BELL-VE-DEER

HAT FOR
SKINNY MINNIE

CUT ONE 8″-DIAMETER CIRCLE
(PINKED EDGES PREFERRED).

ANTLER

CUT TWO.

(NOTE: Body, legs, and arms for Bell-ve-deer are
from one pair of white terry-lined work
socks. See pages 53-55.)

PLACE ON FOLD.

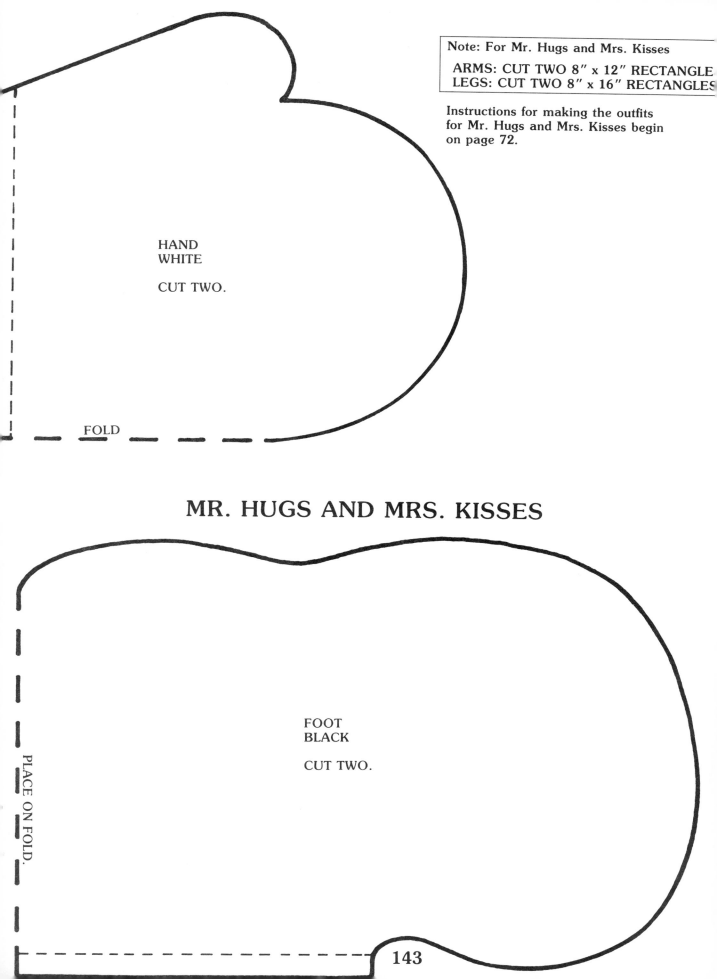

HAND
WHITE

CUT TWO.

FOLD

Note: For Mr. Hugs and Mrs. Kisses

ARMS: CUT TWO 8″ x 12″ RECTANGLE
LEGS: CUT TWO 8″ x 16″ RECTANGLES

Instructions for making the outfits
for Mr. Hugs and Mrs. Kisses begin
on page 72.

MR. HUGS AND MRS. KISSES

FOOT
BLACK

CUT TWO.

PLACE ON FOLD.

BLOOMERS

CUT TWO.

TOP

FOLD

APRON

CUT ONE.

Marketing

Q. *Are you one of those successful people who always knew just what she wanted to do and worked according to a plan to achieve predetermined goals?*

A.   Goodness, no. As a youngster, I dreamed of someday becoming a fashion designer. I loved the challenge of perfecting new designs. Then I met Larry and decided to expand my career goals to become a wife and mother. I sewed for our two daughters and myself. From the resulting scraps of material and trim, I began to make crude pillow-type dolls for the children to play with. Even though the toys were not especially pretty, our girls loved them. And I got as much pleasure from designing toys as they did from playing with them.

Q. *So then you decided to go into the business?*

A.   Well, not exactly. I was a "milk and cookies" mama and proud of it. I was home every day, baking bread, sewing, being a "good mother" like the role models in the 1950's television shows. Then when our older daughter, Kim, was in the second grade, she wrote a story titled "What My Mommy Does." I was so pleased and could hardly wait to hear her glowing praise. What I heard was, "My mommy doesn't do anything. She's a housewife."

On top of that, just a few days later, the girls excitedly burst in the door from school, thinking we had company. When they saw only dear old Mom, they said, "Huh? Nobody here?" And I could only think, "What am I—chopped liver?"

I guess that's what did it. I realized that I needed to do something with my life for me. I was Larry's wife and Kim and Deanna's mother, but that was all. So I began a journey to become Me.

And even though I was searching for something for myself, my business really stemmed from my love for my family. Who would have thought a young mother who started making her children's toys out of scraps of fabric and trim left over from homemade clothes would someday become a toy designer and the president of a toy company? I had wanted safe, washable toys for my children. The money I saved and the career these toys introduced were just bonuses. Isn't it amazing what love can do?

Q. *If you felt the need to be an "at-home" mother so strongly, how did you accept the changes that must have occurred as you began your business?*

A.   I'm very lucky. My interests and my business are centered around my family. I do much of my work at home, and the whole family like to put their two cents in. When I was working on the Sea Creatures group, Larry, my husband, suggested a starfish, and Deanna provided the idea for its personality. I combined their ideas to design an exotic "queen of the silver sea." Larry named her Star-la Fish. Who said work isn't family fun? Mine is. I'm proud to say, "My work is child's play."

Q. *Surely there were difficulties in converting a hobby to a full-time business.*

A.   Yes, of course, there were. There's a lot of competition out there in the marketplace. A marketable item should have a professional appearance, and that means lots of practice in perfecting an assembly-line approach to making the item.

Costs became greater, too. It was impractical to depend on scraps of fabric for materials. That meant volume buying of supplies used in production. And, naturally, there was the need for more help. As my business grew, I could not continue to "wear all the hats," so I needed to hire employees. And as always with a growing business, we needed more income than we could generate. It takes years before a company can expect to realize any genuine profit.

We started small; I worked at my own pace and set my own hours. Running a business is not something that I learned and succeeded at overnight. Anything worth having takes time and effort. I've spent twenty years developing a by-the-way hobby into a profitable business.

Q. *Did you ever doubt that you would really succeed?*

A.   Let's say that I tried to prepare for success. I studied the market, talked to people in the trade, showed the items I planned to market, and asked for and listened to opinions. It's important to listen to others' ideas with an open mind and with the willingness to take criticism. People who said they loved my toys just because that's what they thought I wanted to hear did me no favors. Of course, I didn't take every bit of advice I was given, but I did listen and consider those ideas.

Doing my homework to learn all I could and believing in what I was doing were critical to my success. I was confident of my ability and the quality of my product, so I hung in there. That was the hardest part but the most important.

Q. *What quality in your toys did other craftsmen seem to admire most when they gave you their opinions and criticism?*

A.   Originality is the key. I try to take patterns and change them to reflect my personality. Each of us is special: our products should be special, too. I've noticed at crafts fairs that the best craftsmen bring a uniqueness to their work that distinguishes theirs from all others in their line. Every excellent craftsman is an innovator, not an imitator.

Q. *Have crafts shows and fairs been particularly helpful to you in achieving success?*

A.   Crafts shows are essential. There are so many of them—large, small, local, regional, national. They're a great way to learn practically everything you need to know. Before I ever participated in a show, I attended as a looker/buyer. I checked the competition in similar media, comparing the quality of materials, construction, design, and price. I observed the displays and presentations. I asked a lot of questions and listened to plenty of answers.

Small, local crafts fairs offer a super opportunity to someone just starting out in business to test his products and try his marketing techniques. Many of these small shows are free to participants, and since so many communities sponsor such events, it's possible to take part in a fair without incurring even travel expenses. Larger shows usually include hundreds of exhibitors, charge fees, and provide substantial publicity. They often involve travel to major cities, but they certainly offer wider exposure. The larger the show, the keener the competition. Crafts fairs are marvelous markets and have given me some of my fondest memories.

Q. *I believe you attend the fairs for pleasure as well as for business!*

A.   I surely do! A crafts fair is a gathering of artistic craftsmen, many items of true museum or art gallery calibre, mothers who can't make up their minds, daddies with headaches, laughing children seeking the best buy for their money, a time to catch up on what's happening, visits with fellow craftsmen, and trading. A crafts show is an experience!

Craftsmen are unique individuals—creative, sharing, caring people who, when they acknowledge you as one of their own, become like family. I look forward to seeing them from year to year at various shows.

My family and I enjoy participating in crafts shows; they are exciting, fun, and educational. We enjoy meeting the customers, hearing their comments, and seeing children's eyes light up when they spot our toys. As a mother, I always design something especially for the children to be able to purchase for a small amount of money. Those designs are not made for profit; they are made for love. Besides having the children's shopping corner, I have always tried to provide something for everyone and for every pocketbook—a wide variety of designs and prices.

Q. *You make these shows sound like such fun that you must want to go to as many as possible.*

A.   You'd better believe it. But don't think it's been a bed of roses all along. Can you imagine what it's like to sew all year, trying to make enough toys to appear in *one* crafts show, filled with excitement and just *knowing* you're going to sell out within the first thirty minutes? Then you sit there for four days. Your smile wears thin. (Smiles are required.) You wonder, "Why aren't they buying these lovely creations?" You get miffed. "Well, these people don't know quality when they see it." You want to pack up and go home, but there's a rule that no one can start packing before the last day of the show unless he wants to be disqualified from the next year's show.

An unsuccessful crafts show is a good learning experience. What will you do with merchandise not sold at a show? Will you store everything until next year? Can you find other outlets? Were your goals unrealistic? It's important to take time to rethink the situation.

It's especially helpful to consider your prices. Prices too high or too low can mean trouble. People are willing to pay more for quality and originality, yet it's possible to price yourself out of the market. A price that's too low may cause people to think your item is of inferior quality. You certainly can't "give your items away." Even though you may have used scraps and not experienced any cost in the production, your *time* is valuable, and the scraps will have to be replaced with *bought* fabric. So it's important to keep track of the hours spent and supplies used, for these must be figured into the cost of your product.

Q. *You mentioned the need for a craftsman to find other outlets besides crafts shows. What other ways have you sold your toys?*

A.   Consignment is a method that can work well. Basically, the craftsman provides the product for a shop and gets paid when the shop sells that item. Consignment checks are usually sent once a month for sales made during the previous month. The shop adds a percentage to the artist's asking price, usually 20-40%. Consignment shops that are well established and selective about the quality of products they carry can do a very good job in marketing. Before entering into an agreement with a shop, it's important to find out how the owners plan to display your product and how they handle stolen or broken merchandise.

As my business has grown, I've begun wholesale selling, too. In plain talk, wholesaling means selling a product at one-half the retail value. Volume sales mean I'm often expected to make hundreds or thousands of one item. For this stage of marketing, help is usually necessary for production as well as for other facets of the business. There is a time frame, from time of order to delivery date, that we must work within. Cost of production and other expenses must be carefully figured, as the profit is smaller per item, relying on volume sales. Quality must be consistent. Marketing in this manner is not for beginners in business.

Q. *You've mentioned the crafts fairs, consignment selling, and wholesaling to present your toys to the public. Do you not have a need to advertise?*

A.   One rule of any business, large or small, is ADVERTISE. Let the public know you have something for sale. I place ads in the local paper and shopping guide. For seasonal items, which toys often are, I place ads in September and October to bring in Christmas orders which I'll have enough time to fill. Some people even place signs in their yards.

And each toy we sell carries a small card bearing the name of our company and the address. All craftsmen should identify their products in such a way. The card may be individually written or run off on a copy machine. Lettering may be done by hand or machine. How it is done doesn't matter just as long as it is neat and concise. That little card is working to inform others about who made that product, and it may bring in future sales.

Q. *Clearly you are a smart businesswoman. Do you feel different from chopped liver now?*
A.   All I wanted was to be someone my family could be proud of. Now we have a company that we're all a part of. We have joyful memories and happy successes that we've shared. That's not bad!

Nobody has to feel like chopped liver. I hope this book will encourage everyone who reads it to try to achieve what is in his heart. The experience will be heartwarming.